Real Food
for your
Baby

Catherine Atkinson

foulsham
LONDON • NEW YORK • TORONTO • SYDNEY

foulsham

The Publishing House, Bennetts Close,
Cippenham, Berks, SL1 5AP, England

ISBN 0-572-02622-6

Printed in Great Britain by The Bath Press, Bath

CONTENTS

INTRODUCTION

Weaning is the gradual process of introducing solid food to a baby who has relied entirely on milk or milk formula. It's an important and rewarding stage in your baby's development, but can also be a frustrating and confusing time: when it comes to feeding babies, the world seems to be full of people giving conflicting advice on what, when and how!

In this book you'll find plenty of help to guide you through the next 12 months or so, from those first few spoonfuls to the point when your child will be joining in family meals. Your baby's progress will be gradual, starting with baby rice with a consistency only slightly thicker than milk, moving on to thin, smooth purées. As your baby grows, you will find you no longer need to purée the food and can mash it with a fork, then later simply chop into small pieces. The chapters reflect this and are divided into the different stages of weaning, so you can take it step by step. Most of the recipes are quick and simple to prepare and can be made in larger quantities so that several portions can be frozen for future use.

Cooking for a baby can be fun, as well as being a healthier and cost-effective alternative to bland, processed meals from jars or packets. By serving a wide range of fresh, home-made food, you can help develop your baby's tastebuds to appreciate a variety of foods, flavours and textures throughout childhood and beyond. Remember that first impressions are lasting, and that applies to first foods too!

Throughout the book, you will find I have referred to the baby as 'she' – simply because all the recipes have been tried and tested over the years by my daughters, Harriet and Liz.

THE BEST FOOD FOR YOUR BABY

Babies have very different nutritional needs from adults. Their need for energy and protein is high in relation to their size during this stage of rapid growth and development. Forget about low-fat, high-fibre foods; they're great for adults, but are not suitable for babies as they may fill their stomachs up before they can absorb all the nutrients they need.

Babies need as varied a diet as possible. Give your baby plenty of carbohydrate foods such as rice, pasta, bread and cereals (but not the high-fibre varieties), vitamin-rich fruit and vegetables and a good helping of protein-rich foods such as meat, fish, eggs and dairy produce. Although fats and oils contain the essential fat-soluble vitamins A, D, E and K, don't add more than is necessary when preparing foods as your baby will get enough of these from foods such as meat and dairy produce. Most babies and children (and adults!) have a sweet tooth, but try to avoid sugary foods where possible, as these have little nutritional value, and never add salt to baby food, as their kidneys are too immature to cope with it.

Although most babies are born with adequate stores of iron, these are used up by the age of about six months, so it's important to provide some iron-rich foods in the diet. Iron is found in concentrated amounts in meat and other foods, including egg yolks and, to a lesser extent, in pulses. Breakfast cereals and follow-on milk formula are also good sources as most are fortified with iron. Vitamin C helps the body to absorb iron, so offer vitamin-rich fruit and vegetables with or immediately after your baby's meals.

Vitamin drops are sometimes recommended for breast-fed babies and bottle-fed babies who are having less than 500 ml/ 17 fl oz/2¼ cups of milk formula daily. Ask your health visitor for advice on this.

WEANING FROM MILK FEEDS TO SOLIDS

During the first few months, breast or formula milk has provided all the nutrients babies need to grow and develop. But between four and six months they need more iron and other nutrients than can be provided by milk alone and may be ready to start on solids.

Signs that show your baby is ready for solids:

◇ Your baby still seems hungry after a milk feed and you've tried giving more milk.

◇ Your baby starts to demand feeds more frequently.

◇ Having started to sleep through the night, your baby starts waking again for a feed.

◇ Your baby seems interested in the food that you're eating and puts objects into her mouth to feel and chew.

Be guided by your own baby; if she's showing some or all of these signs, it's probably time to start giving solids. Babies progress at different rates and a few large babies may need to start earlier than four months, but this is unusual. Check with your health visitor if you have any worries about when to start. Don't be pressurised by friends or relatives into starting sooner; you'll meet other parents who see weaning as a competition and believe that the sooner the better. Remember that a baby's digestive system is not fully matured in the first few months and that giving solids too early increases the chances of allergies later on. On the other hand, babies start to learn how to chew at around six months, so don't delay giving solids after this age, or your baby may find it difficult to learn this skill.

GETTING STARTED

When you start giving your baby solid food you are simply introducing different tastes and textures and getting her used to feeding from a spoon. She still relies on her milk feeds for nourishment.

At first, offer food only once a day and introduce just one taste at a time. Baby rice cereal is an ideal first food as it's easy to digest. When mixed with breast or formula milk, the familiar taste and smell will help your baby relate to this new food. After a week or so, you can move on to fruit and mild-tasting vegetable purées. Apart from ripe bananas, these should always be cooked until very tender. At the beginning of weaning, food should have a very smooth, runny consistency, so you may need to thin purées with baby milk (breast or formula) or cooled, boiled water to achieve this.

When you introduce solids for the first time, choose a feed when your baby is alert and hungry but without being frantic; towards midday after a morning nap is usually a good choice. Give her a small milk feed to settle her and just take the edge off her hunger, then offer the solid food. Finish with the rest of the milk feed. Alternatively, you can try at the end of the milk feed if this works better.

At the beginning, the quantity of solids needed is minute – don't expect your baby to take more than a teaspoonful as her digestive system is still very immature. Remember, though, that you'll need to prepare at least double this amount as a lot of food will be dribbled straight back out rather than swallowed. Gradually build up the amount to 10–15 ml/ 2–3 tsp of food and when your baby happily takes one meal a day, you can move on to two meals a day.

INTRODUCING SOLID FOOD

Before starting to feed your baby, check that the food is at the right temperature. It should be just lukewarm; if it's too hot, you could put her off eating before she's tried her first spoonful! Next, protect your baby with a bib and have a damp flannel or kitchen paper (paper towels) to hand. Sit your baby upright in your lap, cradling her in your arm, so that she feels safe and secure. Later, when she's used to feeding, you may find it easier to feed her in a portable car seat or a bouncy baby chair on the floor. When she can sit up at about six or seven months, you can strap her into a highchair.

WEANING TIPS

◇ Scoop up a tiny amount of food on a small, plastic, sterilised spoon and gently place it between your baby's lips. Don't put the spoon in too far or she may gag.

◇ A lot of the food will probably be dribbled straight out again; it takes time to learn to feed from a spoon. Gently scrape it up and try again!

◇ If your baby doesn't like taking food from a spoon, try dipping a clean finger into the food and letting her suck the food off it.

◇ Go at your baby's pace, which will be slow. When she's had enough, she'll turn her head away.

◇ When your baby has finished, sit with her for a few minutes, keeping her in an upright position.

◇ If your baby is very reluctant to take solid foods and becomes upset, don't worry. Go back to breast or bottle feeding and try again in a few days, time.

◇ Never force your baby to take more food than she wants.

BUYING EQUIPMENT TO GET STARTED

A visit to your local baby shop may make you think that you need masses of special equipment for weaning your baby. In fact, you need very little, especially for the first few weeks, and you'll probably already have most of it in your kitchen.

THE ESSENTIALS

Plastic spoons You'll find spoons intended for weaning in baby-care shops and chemists. Babies can't lick food off a spoon at first, so these should be smooth with a shallow bowl that won't hurt your baby's gums.

Bibs Start with several fabric bibs with a plastic backing, the larger the better (puréed carrot goes a long way and stains badly!). When your baby sits up, you may prefer to use an easy-to-wash plastic 'pelican' bib with a trough to catch spills. Bibs with sleeves are also available for older babies who are starting to feed themselves.

Training beakers with a fitted lid and leakproof spout These are invaluable. A huge range is available: some have an interchangeable teat and spout, which is helpful when you want your baby to move on from a bottle to a drinking cup.

Plastic chopping boards These are better than wooden ones, which may harbour germs.

Fine plastic or stainless steel sieve (strainer) This is useful for removing pips and skins from puréed or mashed food.

Small heavy-based saucepan with a lid A small, good-quality pan is vital for cooking small quantities of food with minimal liquid.

Highchair When your baby is about six months old and her neck and back muscles are strong enough to support her, a high chair will make feeding much easier. Shop around to find one that meets your needs. Many will fold up to save space, others convert to a table and chair to be used when your baby becomes a toddler. Choose a model with a washable, non-fabric seat and tray; those with raised edges will catch any spills. Make sure that it is stable, with a secure safety harness, or hooks where one can be attached, to prevent your child from climbing out. If you buy secondhand, check carefully for wear and tear. Where space (and money) is at a premium, you may prefer to opt for a clip-on chair that can be attached to a table or work surface. When your child is over 18 months, a booster seat strapped to an ordinary chair will allow her to reach the table and will make her feel a lot more grown-up!

THE EXTRAS

Hand-held blender or liquidiser Although a fork or masher and a sieve (strainer) are perfectly adequate for making baby purées, an electric machine makes the job a lot quicker and easier, although you will still have to sieve some foods after puréeing to remove skins and pips. If you're buying new, choose one that can purée small quantities of food; family-sized blenders are designed to deal with large quantities and if you're only processing a small amount, the mixture tends to get stuck under the blades. A hand-turned food mill with fine and coarse cutting discs is a good alternative, as it purées the food and separates it from the skin and pips.

Steam steriliser or a cold solution Bottles and spoons can be sterilised in boiling water (see below), but a cold solution – where bottles and equipment are submerged in cold water and sterilising solution – or a steam steriliser is a good investment and easier to use.

Face cloths or baby wipes These are hygienic and handy for wiping sticky faces and hands (and other places where the food has reached!).

Plastic mat If you can't place the highchair on a floor that can be mopped clean, a mat is useful for catching any spills. Sheets of newspaper work just as well, with the added bonus that they can simply be rolled up afterwards and thrown away.

FOOD HYGIENE

Scares about food poisoning and newspaper-reported cases of salmonella and listeria have made parents especially aware of the importance of basic hygiene. Young babies pick up infections easily, but this can be prevented by following a few common-sense precautions when preparing food.

◇ Always wash your hands with hot water and soap before handling food or feeding equipment – an anti-bacterial handwash is ideal for this.

◇ It's important to continue sterilising bottles and teats until they are no longer used – warm milk is a wonderful breeding ground for bacteria. You may feel that once your baby has started picking up things and putting them in her mouth it is pointless sterilising feeding equipment, but it's a good idea to sterilise feeding spoons and drinking beakers until your baby is a year old. This can be achieved by boiling in a saucepan of water for 25 minutes, by immersing in a container of cold water with sterilising fluid or tablets, or in a steam steriliser, following the manufacturers instructions.

◇ It's impossible to sterilise all large equipment. Use a dishwasher if you have one, as it washes at a higher temperature than you can achieve by handwashing. Otherwise, wash feeding bowls, sieves (strainers), blenders, etc. by hand in soapy water, rinsing in clean hot water.

Leave to air-dry in a rack, or use a clean tea towel (dish cloth) or kitchen paper (paper towels). Scald larger items such as chopping boards and knives with boiling water before using.

◇ Keep your kitchen work surfaces, chopping boards and utensils (choose plastic rather than wooden) scrupulously clean.

◇ If you have a pet, keep a separate can opener, fork and dish for its food and wash them up separately.

◇ Cool baby food as quickly as possible; putting the bowl or pan in a sink of iced water that comes about halfway up the container will chill it quickly. Cover and refrigerate or freeze as soon the food is cool.

COOKING AND FREEZING BABY FOOD

Cooking tiny amounts of food for your baby can be frustrating, so where possible, prepare extra portions and freeze for later use. There are just a few foods that don't freeze well, such as bananas and avocados, and this is indicated at the end of each of the recipes in the following chapters.

In the first few months, freeze portions in sterilised ice cube trays; one cube will be enough for each meal and as your baby's appetite increases you can use two or three cubes. After spooning the purée into the ice cube trays, open-freeze until solid, then press out into plastic bags, tying and labelling with the food and date before returning to the freezer.

To thaw a meal, remove the required number of food cubes required and allow to defrost at room temperature in a covered bowl. Heat until piping hot, then allow to cool to the desired serving temperature; always test before serving. Never reheat more than once or refreeze thawed food.

FREEZER STORAGE TIMES
(in a freezer at −18°C/0°F)

Purées containing milk	6 weeks
Meat, chicken and fish	2 months
Fruit and vegetables	4 months

APPROXIMATE AGES FOR INTRODUCING NEW FOODS

Introduce new foods gradually so that your baby has a chance to get used to different tastes.

AT FOUR MONTHS

Baby rice
Cooked apple, papaya (pawpaw), pear
Ripe banana
Cooked carrots, courgette (zucchini), marrow (squash), parsnip, potato, squash, swede (rutabaga)

AT FIVE MONTHS

Non-wheat cereals, such as barley, oats, rye, soya
Kiwi fruit, melon, plums, raspberries
Spinach, celery, peas, leeks, sweetcorn (corn), cabbage, mushrooms, cauliflower, broccoli
Lentils and well-cooked pulses

AT SIX MONTHS

Soaked dried fruit, such as apricots and peaches (but avoid raisins and sultanas (golden raisins))
Strawberries (see Allergies and food intolerance, page 16)
Tomatoes
Full-fat cows' milk in cooking
Dairy products, such as mild cheese, yoghurt, fromage frais
Tofu
White poultry meat, such as chicken and turkey
White fresh or frozen fish, such as cod, plaice and haddock
Cocoa (unsweetened chocolate) powder

AT SEVEN MONTHS

Pasta
Bread, breadsticks, crispbread, rusks
Citrus fruit
Fingers of cooked vegetables such as carrot
Cooked egg yolk
Lean red meat: beef and lamb

AT NINE MONTHS

Cooked whole eggs
Soaked raisins and sultanas (golden raisins)
Finely ground nuts (see Allergies and food intolerance, page 16)
Oily and canned fish, such as sardines, mackerel, salmon and tuna
Sticks of raw fruit and vegetables

AT ONE YEAR

Shellfish (see Allergies and food intolerance, page 16)
Honey
Smooth peanut butter (see Allergies and food intolerance, page 16)

AT THREE YEARS

Whole nuts (see Allergies and food intolerance, page 16)

MILK MATTERS

In the early stages of weaning, breast or formula milk will continue to provide most of the nutrients your baby needs and you should still be giving her at least 600 ml/1 pint/2½ cups a day, or four feeds if you are breastfeeding. As you continue with mixed feeding, your baby will gradually demand fewer milk feeds, but milk will still be an important part of the diet. By the age of six months, most babies are able to sip, rather than just suck, so start offering milk in a lidded feeder cup with meals at this time. You can breastfeed for as long as you want, but encourage your baby to give up the bottle by the age of one year, or the habit becomes very hard to break.

The UK Department of Health recommends that babies continue to have breast or formula milk throughout their first year. Follow-on milk formula can be introduced at six months and contains iron in a form that can be easily absorbed as well as vital vitamins. Cows' milk should not be given as a main drink before the age of one year because it contains only small amounts of iron and vitamin D and proteins that some babies find hard to digest. It can, however, be used in cooking from six months.

Specially modified soya infant formulas are available for

babies who have problems digesting breast or ordinary formula milk. They should only ever be given if advised by your doctor and you'll also need to speak to your dentist as their sugar content has been known to cause the developing teeth to decay.

When your child is about one year old, you can switch to full-fat (silver top) cows' milk. Aim to give a minimum of 350 ml/⅔ pint/1½ cups a day. For children who won't drink milk, give two servings of dairy products, such as cheese, fromage frais, yoghurt or milky desserts. After the age of two, you can swap to semi-skimmed milk if you prefer, provided your child is eating and growing satisfactorily. Skimmed milk is not suitable for children under five, as it is too low in calories and does not contain the fat-soluble vitamins A and D.

OTHER DRINKS

Always make sure that your baby has enough to drink, especially when the weather is hot. You can give water as well as milk. For babies under six months, tap water should always be boiled, then cooled. You can also give bottled water (avoid those labelled 'natural mineral waters') but this should also be boiled and cooled first. Do not give your baby carbonated, softened, or repeatedly boiled water because of the concentration of mineral salts.

At six months, you can start to introduce unsweetened fruit juice, such as apple or orange, diluting one part juice with three parts water and gradually increasing to half and half. These should be offered with, rather than between, meals as the fruit acids are harmful to the teeth. Some drinks manufactured specifically for babies and also many squashes contain surprising amounts of added sugar and should be avoided before the age of one. Check the label for sucrose, glucose, fructose, dextrose, maltose and honey – these are all forms of sugar.

COMMERCIALLY PREPARED FOOD

Although the emphasis of this book is that 'fresh is best', there are times when you'll find that pre-prepared jars, cans and packets of baby food are simply more convenient, especially when you're away from home. Dried baby foods are often useful during the early stages of weaning when you only need tiny amounts of food. Don't feel guilty about serving commercially prepared baby food when it suits you, but make sure your baby still gets variety and try to include plenty of fresh home-made food as well.

VEGETARIAN BABIES

A growing baby can get all the necessary nutrients from a diet excluding meat and fish, but it's important to balance the diet to ensure she gets enough protein, vitamins B12 and D, calcium and iron. Your baby can get plenty of protein from eggs, pulses, milk and dairy products including vegetarian cheese, tofu, finely ground nuts and nut spreads (see Allergies and food intolerance, page 16). When she is over six months, puréed dried fruits, such as apricots, and fortified breakfast cereals, will provide iron in the diet. Vegetarian diets tend to be higher in fibre and therefore bulkier than those containing meat, so serve high-protein, low-fibre foods such as eggs and cheese daily.

If you choose to bring up your baby as a vegan and exclude all dairy foods and eggs from her diet, ask your doctor or health visitor to refer you to a dietitian for specialist advice.

Whatever type of diet you decide on, have your baby weighed regularly at a health clinic; it'll reassure you that she's growing well and give you the chance to talk about any feeding problems.

ALLERGIES AND FOOD INTOLERANCE

Allergic reactions to food are extremely rare, but it's important to be aware of the symptoms, especially if there is a history of allergies in the family, as the results can be serious. The first noticeable reactions are usually red blotches on the skin and swelling of the face, eyes, mouth and tongue, often followed by nausea, vomiting and diahorrea.

The allergen – the substance in the food that caused the reaction – may only produce very mild symptoms the first time the food is eaten, but if the child is repeatedly given the food, the symptoms will become increasingly severe. It's therefore important to introduce new foods one at a time and preferably at breakfast or lunchtime rather than last thing at night, so that you will immediately be aware of any problems should they occur. If your child's mouth and tongue start to swell almost immediately after a trying a new food, seek medical help without delay.

Certain foods, like gluten which is found in wheat, are more likely to cause reactions. Others potential allergens are egg whites, nuts (especially peanuts), sesame seeds, shellfish, strawberries and cows' milk.

Food intolerance differs from an allergy and occurs when the digestive system doesn't produce the enzymes necessary to break down a certain food in the body. The most common is lactose intolerance – the inability to digest the sugars in milk due to an absence of the enzyme lactase. The enzyme may be absent at birth, or sometimes production of the enzyme stops after an illness such as gastroenteritis. If diagnosed, your doctor will advise you to switch to a soya milk formula. Some children who have an intolerance to lactose will still be able to eat dairy products such as yoghurt and cheese.

MAKING MEAL TIMES EASY

The meal planners in the subsequent chapters aim to help you through the early weeks and months of weaning, but are intended as a guide only; there's no need to follow them rigidly – you can swap meals around or leave out certain foods as you wish. Don't feel that you have to prepare every meal for baby from scratch; save time and energy by making use of some of the vegetables you've cooked for the rest of the family – a few steamed carrots or a baked potato – but if you wish to add salt or strong spices to your food, remember to remove a portion for your baby first. Offering your baby home-made food will get her used to the food that the rest of the family eats, making things easier when it comes to joining in family meal times.

It's a good idea to serve the same food for two consecutive days, so that the baby can get used to each new flavour before introducing a new one – babies don't mind repetition, after all they've lived on milk alone for several months. If your baby rejects any new food with obvious dislike, go back to serving the foods she enjoys and try the new food again at a later date. Never make eating a battleground; just like adults, babies have likes and dislikes.

NOTES ON THE RECIPES

◇ All spoon measures are level: 1 tsp = 5 ml;
1 tbsp = 15 ml.

◇ Ingredients are given in metric, imperial and American measures. Use only one set per recipe; do not interchange.

◇ Ensure that all produce is as fresh as possible.

◇ Always wash, peel, core and seed, if necessary, fresh fruit and vegetables before use.

◇ Avoid adding salt for babies or using ready-made products that are high in salt, such as some stock cubes.

◇ Use fresh herbs unless dried are specifically called for.

◇ All cooking times are approximate and are intended as a guide only.

◇ Always preheat the oven, unless it is a fan-assisted one, and cook on the centre shelf, unless otherwise stated.

◇ The following symbols are used throughout the recipes to denote whether or not a recipe is suitable for freezing:

❋ Suitable for freezing

❀ Not suitable for freezing

ABOUT FOUR MONTHS

These first mini-mouthfuls introduce your baby to a whole new experience in taste and texture. Make it a positive and happy time and she'll learn to see meal times as enjoyable occasions. Start by offering just a teaspoonful or two of baby rice mixed with baby milk (either breast or formula milk, whichever your baby is used to) to the consistency of single cream for the first week, then move on to runny fruit and vegetable purées. Gradually increase this to 10–15 ml/2–3 tsp at each meal and finally to two meals a day.

FOODS TO AVOID AT FOUR MONTHS

◇ Citrus or soft berry fruits – these can cause allergic reactions in some babies

◇ Cows' milk – give breast or formula milk instead

◇ Eggs

◇ Foods containing gluten, found in wheat, as your baby may find them difficult to digest

◇ Meat, poultry, fish and shellfish

◇ Nuts, including peanut butter and sesame seeds

◇ Salt

◇ Stock made from cubes or granules

◇ Sugar or honey – instead, choose naturally sweet, ripe fruit and mild-tasting vegetables such as young carrots and parsnips

FOUR TO FIVE MONTHS MEAL PLANNER

Week	Day	Lunch	Tea
1	Monday–Sunday	Baby rice (page 21)	
2	Monday	Banana purée (page 21)	
	Tuesday	Apple purée (page 21)	
	Wednesday	Apple purée (page 21)	
	Thursday	Carrot purée (page22)	
	Friday	Carrot purée (page22)	
	Saturday	Pear purée (page 22)	
	Sunday	Pear purée (page 22)	
3	Monday	Potato purée (page 23)	Banana purée (page 21)
	Tuesday	Banana purée (page 21)	Potato purée (page 23)
	Wednesday	Swede (rutabaga) purée (page 23)	Banana purée (page 21)
	Thursday	Cream of fruit purée (page 22)	Swede (rutabaga) purée (page 23)
	Friday	Butternut squash purée (page 24)	Cream of fruit purée (page 22)
	Saturday	Papaya (pawpaw) purée (page 22)	Butternut squash purée (page 24)
	Sunday	Parsnip purée (page23)	Papaya (pawpaw) purée (page 22)
4	Monday	Two-fruit purée (page 23)	Potato purée (page 23)
	Tuesday	Carrot purée (page 23)	Two-fruit purée (page 23)
	Wednesday	Apple purée (page 22)	Carrot purée (page 23)
	Thursday	Apple purée (page 21)	Parsnip purée (page 23)
	Friday	Pear purée (page 22)	Swede (rutabaga) purée (page 23)
	Saturday	Potato purée (page 23)	Pear purée (page 22)
	Sunday	Cream of fruit purée (page 23)	Potato purée (page 23)

COOKING PURÉES IN THE MICROWAVE

Apple, pear and vegetable purées can be cooked in a microwave if preferred. Put the sliced or diced fruit or vegetable in a bowl with 15 ml/1 tbsp of water. Cover with clingfilm (plastic wrap), pierce in several places and cook on High for 5–6 minutes or until very tender. Purée, cool and serve as before.

BABY RICE

MAKES I BABY PORTION

Most baby rice cereals are fortified with vitamins and all should be salt- and sugar-free, but it's worth checking the packet to make sure. Spoon 10 ml/2 tsp of rice into a sterilised bowl. Stir in sufficient baby milk (breast or formula), according to packet instructions, to make a smooth runny consistency. Check the temperature before feeding – it should be barely warm.

BANANA PURÉE

MAKES I BABY PORTION

Mash a 5 cm/2 in piece of very ripe banana with a fork to make it as smooth as possible, or press through a very fine sieve (strainer). Stir in 10–15 ml/2–3 tsp baby milk (breast or formula) or cooled, boiled water to make a runny consistency. Serve straight away.

APPLE PURÉE

MAKES 4 BABY PORTIONS

Peel, quarter and core 1 sweet eating (dessert) apple. Slice thinly and put in a small saucepan with 15 ml/1 tbsp of apple juice or water. Cover and simmer gently for 10 minutes or until very soft. Purée in a blender or press through a fine sieve (strainer). Spoon a quarter into a serving bowl and leave until tepid before serving. Cool the remainder and freeze in portions, or cover and store in the fridge for up to 24 hours.

PEAR PURÉE

MAKES 4 BABY PORTIONS

Peel, quarter and core 1 ripe pear. Chop and put in a small saucepan with 15 ml/1 tbsp of water. Cover and simmer gently for 7–8 minutes or until very soft. Purée in a blender or press through a fine sieve (strainer). Spoon one-quarter into a serving bowl and leave until tepid before serving. Cool the remainder and freeze in portions, or cover and store in the fridge for up to 24 hours.

PAPAYA (PAWPAW) PURÉE

MAKES 3 BABY PORTIONS

Thickly peel and remove the black seeds from ¼ ripe papaya (pawpaw). Put in a steamer or a sieve (strainer), placed over a pan of boiling water. Cover with a lid and steam for 3–4 minutes until very soft. Purée in a blender until smooth or press through a fine sieve. Spoon one-third into a serving bowl and leave until tepid before serving. Cool the remainder and freeze in portions, or cover and store in the fridge for up to 24 hours.

CREAM OF FRUIT PURÉE

MAKES I BABY PORTION

Mix 5 ml/1 tsp of baby rice with 10 ml/2 tsp of baby milk (breast or formula) or cooled, boiled water. Stir in 15 m/1 tbsp of apple, pear or papaya (pawpaw) purée.

TWO-FRUIT PURÉE

MAKES I BABY PORTION

Mash a 5 cm/2 in piece of very ripe banana with a fork until smooth or press through a very fine sieve (strainer). Stir in 15 ml/1 tbsp of apple, pear or papaya (pawpaw) purée (see pages 21 and 22) and a little cooled, boiled water, if needed, to make a runny consistency. Serve straight away.

CARROT, SWEDE OR PARSNIP PURÉE

MAKES 4 BABY PORTIONS

❋

Trim and peel 100 g/4 oz of carrot, swede (rutabaga) or parsnip, then cut the vegetables into 2 cm/¾ in dice. Cook in a steamer or a sieve (strainer), placed over a pan of boiling water, for 10–12 minutes until very soft. Purée in a blender or press though a fine sieve. Spoon one-quarter into a serving bowl and leave to cool until tepid. Before serving, stir in enough baby milk (breast or formula) or cooled, boiled water to make the purée the desired consistency. Cool the remainder and freeze in portions, or cover and store in the fridge for up to 24 hours.

POTATO PURÉE

MAKES 4 BABY PORTIONS

❋

Wash a 100 g/4 oz potato and put it in a small saucepan. Barely cover the potato with boiling water and simmer for about 20 minutes until tender. Remove from the water and leave until it is cool enough to handle. Peel off the skin and mash until smooth. Add enough baby milk (breast or formula) to make the purée the desired consistency. Spoon one-quarter into a serving bowl and leave until tepid before serving. Cool the remainder and freeze in portions, or cover and store in the fridge for up to 24 hours.

Alternatively, the potato can be baked in a preheated oven at 200°C/400°F/gas mark 6 for about 1 hour or in the microwave on High for about 5 minutes until tender. Cut in half and scoop out the flesh. Mash as before.

BUTTERNUT SQUASH PURÉE

MAKES 2 BABY PORTIONS

❄

Peel and scoop out the seeds from 100 g/4 oz of butternut squash. Cut the flesh into 2.5 cm/1 in cubes and place in a steamer, or in a sieve (strainer) over a pan of boiling water. Cook for 7–8 minutes or until very tender. Purée in a blender or press through a fine sieve. Spoon half into a serving bowl and leave until tepid before serving. Cool the remainder and freeze, or cover and store in the fridge for up to 24 hours.

ABOUT FIVE MONTHS

By now your baby should be taking (or soon will be) three small solid meals a day and is ready for a slightly more adventurous diet. She may now eat a wider variety of fruit and vegetables with the addition of poultry and fish. Food should still be puréed until smooth, but can be slightly thicker than before. New foods should be introduced at breakfast or lunch-time and it's a good idea to serve them for two consecutive days so that your baby becomes familiar with them and if there is a reaction to a food you will know what caused it.

Make the last meal of the day high in carbohydrates: baby rice and mashed banana are ideal choices as they're easily digested and release energy slowly, and so should help prevent your baby waking through hunger in the night!

When you reach the end of two weeks, simply start at the beginning again and repeat the meals for another two weeks.

FOODS TO AVOID AT FIVE MONTHS

◇ Citrus fruits

◇ Cows' milk

◇ Eggs

◇ Foods containing gluten, found in wheat, including bread and some cereals

◇ Honey, as this may contain botulism bacteria

◇ Nuts, including peanut butter and sesame seeds

◇ Red meat and shellfish

◇ Salty and spicy foods

FIVE TO SIX MONTH MEAL PLANNER

Day	Breakfast	Lunch	Tea
Week 1			
Monday	Creamed rice with apple (page 32)	Autumn vegetable trio (page 28)	Low-sugar rusk mashed with baby milk
Tuesday	Creamed rice with apple (page 32)	Autumn vegetable trio (page 28)	Mashed banana
Wednesday	Banana and kiwi fruit (page 33)	Cream of pumpkin (page 32)	Baby rice cereal mixed with baby milk
Thursday	Apple and raspberry purée (page 33)	Cream of pumpkin (page 32)	Creamed rice with pear purée (page 35)
Friday	Apple and raspberry purée (page 33)	Red lentils with vegetables (page 27)	Creamed rice with pear purée (page 32)
Saturday	Apricot smoothie (page 34)	Red lentils with vegetables (page 27)	Low-sugar rusk mashed with baby milk
Sunday	Apricot smoothie (page 34)	Chicken casserole (pages 28–9)	Mashed banana
Week 2			
Monday	Cream of plum and pear (page 35)	Chicken casserole (pages 28–9)	Baby rice cereal mixed with baby milk
Tuesday	Cream of plum and pear (page 35)	Sweet potato and spinach (page 29)	Low-sugar rusk mashed with baby milk
Wednesday	Blushing fruit salad (page 36)	Sweet potato and spinach (page 29)	Mashed banana
Thursday	Blushing fruit salad (page 36)	Cod and courgette savoury (page 30)	Baby rice cereal mixed with baby milk
Friday	Vanilla peach purée (page 37)	Cod and courgette savoury (page 30)	Low-sugar rusk mashed with baby milk
Saturday	Vanilla peach purée (page 37)	Turkey with peas and sweetcorn (page 31)	Mashed banana
Sunday	Banana and kiwi fruit (page 33)	Turkey with peas and sweetcorn (page 31)	Baby rice cereal mixed with baby milk

RED LENTILS WITH VEGETABLES

MAKES 4 BABY PORTIONS

	METRIC	IMPERIAL	AMERICAN
Red lentils	15 g	½ oz	I tbsp
Small carrot	I	I	I
Cauliflower	100 g	4 oz	4 oz
Potato	100 g	4 oz	4 oz
Formula milk	250 ml	8 fl oz	I cup

① Rinse the lentils thoroughly, discarding any black bits. Trim and peel the vegetables and cut into 2.5 cm/1 in dice.

② Put the lentils and vegetables in a small, heavy-based saucepan with the milk. Bring to the boil, cover and simmer gently for 30 minutes or until the lentils and vegetables are very tender. Check towards the end of the cooking time and top up with a little more milk or boiling water if needed.

③ Purée or sieve (strain) the lentils and vegetables until smooth. Spoon a portion into a bowl and allow to cool, if necessary, before serving.

④ Cool the remaining purée, divide into portions and freeze, or cover and store in the fridge for up to 24 hours.

Tip: The purée will thicken as it cools, so you may need to stir in a little more formula milk before serving.

AUTUMN VEGETABLE TRIO

MAKES 4 BABY PORTIONS

✳	METRIC	IMPERIAL	AMERICAN
Small carrot	I	I	I
Potato	100 g	4 oz	4 oz
Swede (rutabaga)	100 g	4 oz	4 oz
Formula or breast milk	150 ml	¼ pint	⅔ cup

①   Trim and peel the carrot, potato and swede and cut into 2.5 cm/1 in dice. Put the vegetables in a small heavy saucepan and add the milk.

②   Bring the milk to the boil, lower the heat, cover and simmer for 15 minutes or until the vegetables are very soft.

③   Purée or sieve (strain) the vegetables and milk until smooth. Spoon a portion into a bowl and allow to cool, if necessary, before serving.

④   Cool the remaining purée, divide into portions and freeze, or cover and store in the fridge for up to 24 hours.

Tip: Thin the purée with a little extra milk or cooled boiled water if your baby prefers a softer mixture.

CHICKEN CASSEROLE

MAKES 4 BABY PORTIONS

✳	METRIC	IMPERIAL	AMERICAN
Small carrot	I	I	I
Potato	100 g	4 oz	4 oz
Chicken breast, skinned and boned	50 g	2 oz	2 oz
Vegetable stock (page 38) or formula or breast milk	150 ml	¼ pint	⅔ cup

①   Trim and peel the carrot and potato. Cut it into cubes. Cut the chicken into thin strips and put in a small saucepan with the vegetables. Pour in the stock or milk.

②   Bring to the boil, lower the heat, cover and simmer for 15–20 minutes, until the chicken and vegetables are cooked.

③   Purée the mixture until smooth. Spoon a portion into a bowl and allow to cool slightly, if necessary, before serving.

④   Cool the remaining purée, divide into portions and freeze, or cover and store in the fridge for up to 24 hours.

SWEET POTATO AND SPINACH

MAKES 4 BABY PORTIONS

❄	METRIC	IMPERIAL	AMERICAN
Sweet potato	100 g	4 oz	4 oz
Formula or breast milk	150 ml	¼ pint	⅔ cup
Fresh baby spinach leaves	100 g	4 oz	4 oz

①   Peel and rinse the sweet potato and cut it into even-sized pieces. Put in a small saucepan with the milk. Bring to the boil, lower the heat, cover and simmer for 10 minutes.

②   Meanwhile, thoroughly wash the spinach leaves. Remove the excess water in a salad spinner or by patting dry with kitchen paper (paper towels). Remove the stalks.

③   Put the spinach on top of the sweet potato in the pan, cover and cook for a further 8–10 minutes or until the potato and spinach are both very tender.

④   Mash the mixture together until smooth, then press through a sieve (strainer). Spoon a portion into a bowl and allow to cool slightly, if necessary, before serving.

⑤   Cool the remaining purée, divide into portions and freeze, or cover and store in the fridge for up to 24 hours.

COD AND COURGETTE SAVOURY

Cooking fish in foil seals in all the juices and flavour. This is a great way to serve fish and if cooking for the rest of the family, use cod cutlets and simply add a slice of lemon and a sprig or two of dill, parsley or thyme to their portions.

MAKES 4 BABY PORTIONS

❋	METRIC	IMPERIAL	AMERICAN
Cod fillet, skinned	75 g	3 oz	3 oz
Small courgette (zucchini)	1	1	1
Vegetable stock (page 38)	45 ml	3 tbsp	3 tbsp
Butter or margarine	2.5 ml	½ tsp	½ tsp

① Trim the courgette and cut it into thin slices. Put the fish on a piece of foil, scatter over the courgette, then spoon over the stock. Top with the butter or margarine.

② Bring the edges of the foil together and fold over to seal and make a parcel. Place on a baking (cookie) sheet.

③ Bake in a preheated oven at 180°C/350°F/gas mark 4 for 20 minutes or until the fish is cooked and the courgette is tender.

④ Flake the fish with a fork, removing any bones, then purée with the courgette and juices until smooth. Spoon a portion into a bowl and allow to cool slightly, if necessary, before serving.

⑤ Cool the remaining purée, divide into portions and freeze, or cover and store in the fridge for up to 24 hours.

Tip: Add a little more stock or formula or breast milk, if necessary, to make the purée the desired consistency.

TURKEY WITH PEAS AND SWEETCORN

MAKES 4 BABY PORTIONS

	METRIC	IMPERIAL	AMERICAN
Potato	100 g	4 oz	4 oz
Turkey breast, skinned and boned	50 g	2 oz	2 oz
Formula or breast milk	150 ml	¼ pint	⅔ cup
Frozen peas	25 g	1 oz	1 oz
Frozen or canned sweetcorn (corn)	25 g	1 oz	1 oz

① Peel and rinse the potato and chop into even-sized pieces. Cut the turkey into thin strips. Put the potato and turkey into a small saucepan with the milk.

② Bring to the boil, lower the heat, cover and simmer for 10 minutes. Add the peas and sweetcorn and cook for a further 5–10 minutes, until the turkey and vegetables are cooked.

③ Purée the mixture until smooth. Spoon a portion into a bowl and allow to cool slightly, if necessary, before serving.

④ Cool the remaining purée, divide into portions and freeze, or cover and store in the fridge for up to 24 hours.

CREAM OF PUMPKIN

MAKES 4 BABY PORTIONS

❄	METRIC	IMPERIAL	AMERICAN
Pumpkin	100 g	4 oz	4 oz
Baby rice	10 ml	2 tsp	2 tsp
Warm formula or breast milk	120 ml	4 fl oz	½ cup

① Thickly peel the pumpkin and remove the seeds. Cut the flesh into dice, put in a steamer or in a sieve (strainer) over a pan of boiling water and cover with a lid.

② Steam the pumpkin for about 8 minutes or until very tender. Purée in a blender or press through a fine sieve.

③ Mix the baby rice with the milk until smooth. Stir in the pumpkin purée. Spoon a portion into a bowl and allow to cool if necessary.

④ Cool the remainder, divide into portions and freeze, or cover and store in the fridge for up to 24 hours.

CREAMED RICE WITH APPLE

MAKES 2 BABY PORTIONS

❄	METRIC	IMPERIAL	AMERICAN
Sweet eating (dessert) apple	½	½	½
Flaked rice	15 ml	1 tbsp	1 tbsp
Formula or breast milk	100 ml	3½ fl oz	scant ½ cup

① Quarter, core and peel the apple. Slice thinly and put in a small saucepan with the rice and milk.

② Bring to the boil, cover, then simmer very gently for 12–15 minutes, until the apple and rice are cooked, stirring occasionally.

③ Purée the mixture until smooth. Spoon half into a bowl and allow to cool slightly, if necessary, before serving.

④ Cool the remaining purée, cover and store in the fridge for up to 24 hours.

Tip: For Creamed Rice with Pear, replace the apple with pear.

BANANA AND KIWI FRUIT

MAKES 1 BABY PORTION

	METRIC	IMPERIAL	AMERICAN
Ripe banana	¼	¼	¼
Ripe kiwi fruit	¼	¼	¼

① Remove the peel from the banana and kiwi fruit. Mash the banana with a fork until smooth, then push through a fine sieve (strainer).

② Mash the kiwi fruit and push through the sieve to remove the black pips.

③ Mix the two purées together and serve straight away.

APPLE AND RASPBERRY PURÉE

MAKES 4 BABY PORTIONS

	METRIC	IMPERIAL	AMERICAN
Eating (dessert) apple	1	1	1
Apple juice or water	15 ml	1 tbsp	1 tbsp
Fresh or frozen raspberries	25 g	1 oz	1 oz

① Quarter, core, peel and thinly slice the apple. Put in a small saucepan with the apple juice or water.

② Cover and cook over a very low heat for 5 minutes. Add the raspberries and cook for a further 3–4 minutes, until the fruit is very soft, stirring occasionally.

③ Press the mixture through a sieve (strainer) or purée in a blender. If you have used a blender, rub the purée through a sieve to remove the berry pips. Spoon a portion into a bowl and allow to cool slightly, if necessary, before serving.

④ Cool the remaining purée, divide into portions and freeze, or cover and store in the fridge for up to 24 hours.

APRICOT SMOOTHIE

Mixing a more strongly flavoured fruit, such as apricot, with baby rice makes it more palatable when introducing a new taste to your baby.

MAKES 2 BABY PORTIONS

	METRIC	IMPERIAL	AMERICAN
Ripe apricot	1	1	1
Water	5 ml	1 tsp	1 tsp
Baby rice	10 ml	2 tsp	2 tsp
Formula or breast milk	20 ml	4 tsp	4 tsp

① Halve the apricot, discard the stone (pit), then chop the flesh roughly. Put in a small saucepan with the water. Cover and simmer gently for 8 minutes or until the fruit is soft.

② Sieve (strain) the fruit to remove the skin. Blend the baby rice with the milk, then stir in the fruit purée. Spoon a portion into a bowl and allow to cool slightly, if necessary, before serving.

③ Cool the remaining mixture, cover and store in the fridge for up to 24 hours.

Tip: If fresh apricots aren't in season, use 2 canned apricot halves instead, preferably choosing those in natural juice rather than in syrup. They will need cooking for only 2–3 minutes in step 1.

CREAM OF PLUM AND PEAR

MAKES 4 BABY PORTIONS

	METRIC	IMPERIAL	AMERICAN
Ripe plum	I	I	I
Ripe pear	½	½	½
Apple juice or water	10 ml	2 tsp	2 tsp
Low-sugar rusk	½	½	½
Formula or breast milk	30 ml	2 tbsp	2 tbsp

① Peel the plum (see method for Vanilla Peach Purée on page 37 if the skin is difficult to remove). Cut in half and remove the stone (pit). Quarter, core and peel the pear. Roughly chop the fruit and put in a small saucepan with the apple juice or water.

② Cover and simmer gently for 10 minutes, until very soft, stirring occasionally. Sieve (strain) or purée the fruit until smooth.

③ Meanwhile, crumble the rusk into a bowl and sprinkle over the milk. Leave to soften for a few minutes, then mix until smooth. Stir in the fruit purée.

④ Spoon a portion into a bowl and allow to cool slightly, if necessary, before serving.

⑤ Cool the remaining mixture, divide into portions and freeze, or cover and store in the fridge for up to 24 hours.

BLUSHING FRUIT SALAD

MAKES 4 BABY PORTIONS

❋	METRIC	IMPERIAL	AMERICAN
Ripe pear	½	½	½
Apple juice or water	10 ml	2 tsp	2 tsp
Charentais melon	¼	¼	¼
Fresh or frozen raspberries	25 g	1 oz	1 oz

① Quarter, core and peel the pear. Cut into thin slices. Put in a small saucepan with the apple juice or water and simmer gently for 5 minutes.

② Meanwhile, scoop the seeds out of the melon, cut off the skin and dice the flesh. Add to the pan with the raspberries and cook for a further 3–4 minutes, until the fruit is soft.

③ Press the mixture though a sieve (strainer) or purée in a blender and then sieve (strain) to remove the berry pips.

④ Spoon a portion into a bowl and allow to cool slightly, if necessary, before serving. Cool the remaining purée, divide into portions and freeze, or cover and store in the fridge for up to 24 hours.

VANILLA PEACH PURÉE

MAKES 4 BABY PORTIONS

	METRIC	IMPERIAL	AMERICAN
Ripe peach or nectarine	I	I	I
Piece of vanilla pod	2.5 cm	I in	I in
Peach or apple juice or water	15 ml	I tbsp	I tbsp

①   Peel the peach or nectarine. If this is difficult, put in a bowl and cover with boiling water. Remove after 1 minute and rinse under cold water. The skin should come away easily.

②   Halve the fruit, remove the stone (pit), then chop the flesh and put in a small saucepan with the vanilla pod and juice or water. Cover the pan with a lid and cook over a low heat for 10 minutes until the fruit is tender. Remove the vanilla pod.

③   Sieve (strain) or purée the fruit until smooth. Spoon a portion into a bowl and allow to cool slightly, if necessary, before serving.

④   Cool the remaining purée, divide into portions and freeze, or cover and store in the fridge for up to 24 hours.

Tip: Don't throw away the piece of vanilla pod after using. Rinse under cold running water, leave to dry, then store in an airtight container. It can be re-used several times. If you prefer, the peach purée can be made without the vanilla.

HOME-MADE VEGETABLE STOCK

Throughout this and subsequent chapters, you'll find recipes which call for vegetable stock. Don't use commercial stock cubes, granules or powder until your baby is at least nine months old and then only in small amounts, as they contain large quantities of salt. Adding salt puts a strain on the baby's kidneys and encourages a taste for salt, rather than the natural flavour of food, to develop. If you haven't got time to make stock, water may be used in the recipes instead.

MAKES 600 ML/1 PINT/2½ CUPS

❄	METRIC	IMPERIAL	AMERICAN
Onion, peeled	I	I	I
Celery sticks	2	2	2
Carrots, peeled	2	2	2
Water	900 ml	1½ pints	3¾ cups
Bay leaves	2	2	2
A few fresh parsley or thyme sprigs			

① Roughly chop the onion, celery and carrots. Put in a saucepan with the water and herbs.

② Slowly bring to the boil and skim the surface. Part-cover the pan with a lid and simmer for 40 minutes. Leave to cool.

③ Strain the stock through a fine sieve (strainer), discarding the vegetables and herbs. Cover and store in the fridge for up to 3 days or freeze for up to 3 months.

Tip: You'll need different amounts of stock for the recipes, so freeze some 15 ml/1 tbsp portions in ice cube trays and some 150 ml/¼ pint/⅔ cup portions in suitable containers.

SIX TO NINE MONTHS

Your baby can now move on to slightly more textured puréed or mashed food. Try keeping it fairly soft at first, with just a few small lumps, but allow your baby to guide you – some are very resistant to even the tiniest piece! By now she'll have preferences for certain foods and perhaps a few dislikes as well. You can still serve the meals in the previous chapter – choose those which she's familiar with and enjoys, but make them very slightly coarser to get her used to a lumpier texture. There are plenty of new recipes to try in this chapter, but no day-by-day menu planner; it will benefit your baby (and you'll find it a lot easier) if she can start to join in with suitable family meals at this age.

You can use full-fat cows' milk or formula milk in cooking from this age, but stick to formula or breast milk for drinking.

SELF-FEEDING

At around six or seven months, your baby will probably take the first steps towards self-feeding. This is a vital step in her development, so don't discourage her and be prepared to cope with lots of mess to begin with. Gradually she'll become adept at feeding herself and the sooner you start, the quicker you'll reach this stage. She may start grabbing the spoon, so try giving her a second (identical) spoon to hold while you feed her. It will be a couple months, or even longer before she's really able to feed herself, but once she can get the spoon from the bowl and into her mouth, you can help by giving foods that will stick to the spoon rather than slipping straight off – porridge works particularly well. Try introducing a few simple finger foods, such as sticks of lightly cooked vegetables (not raw at this stage) or breadsticks to suck; they encourage independence and will hopefully give you a chance to enjoy your meal. By nine months your baby should be able to cope with a range of finger foods and you'll find a list of these in the next chapter.

When your baby begins to feed herself, eating will take a lot longer, so try to allow for this. Meal times will be seen as a game and this may include playing with and throwing food. She will probably use her fingers, rather than the spoon, at times and enjoy smearing the food around the tray; try to ignore this as long as she is eating as well as playing, but if she's finished eating, remove the food at once. Make it easier on yourself by surrounding the highchair with newspaper. She's also ready now to use a trainer cup by herself. Choose a plastic one that's less likely to break when dropped or thrown, and make sure that the lid is secure.

WHAT TO DO IF YOUR CHILD CHOKES

Never leave your child alone while eating; it's essential that you react quickly if she gags or chokes. If she splutters and gags while eating but can still breathe, reassure her by patting her firmly on the back and talking to her calmly.

If she can't breathe or cough, the windpipe is blocked and you need to take immediate action. Tip her up so that her head is lower than her chest, supporting her head with your forearm and slap firmly between the shoulder blades. If the food is coughed up into her mouth, remove it while her head is still down to prevent re-inhalation. If this does not work, sit the baby up and look down her throat. If you can see the offending object, try to hook it out with your finger (the baby will probably retch, but don't worry as this may help push the trapped object forward). If you're still unsuccessful, don't hesitate to ring for the emergency services, still holding her head downwards.

FOODS TO AVOID FROM SIX TO NINE MONTHS

◇ Egg white

◇ Salty, very spicy and sugary foods, including honey

◇ Shellfish

◇ Nuts, including peanut butter and sesame seeds

MIXED VEGETABLE RISOTTO

MAKES 6 BABY PORTIONS

	METRIC	IMPERIAL	AMERICAN
Long-grain rice	50 g	2 oz	¼ cup
Small red (bell) pepper	¼	¼	¼
Frozen mixed vegetables	25 g	1 oz	1 oz
Milk	300 ml	½ pint	1¼ cups

① Rinse the rice under cold running water and put in a small saucepan. Trim the pepper and dice. Add the pepper and mixed vegetables to the rice and pour in the milk.

② Bring to the boil, part-cover the pan with the lid and simmer for about 12 minutes or until the rice and vegetables are soft.

③ Purée the mixture until fairly smooth. Spoon a portion into a bowl and allow to cool slightly, if necessary, before serving.

④ Cool the remaining purée, divide into portions and freeze, or cover and store in the fridge for up to 24 hours.

CREAMED COD AND CORN CHOWDER

MAKES 6 BABY PORTIONS

❄	METRIC	IMPERIAL	AMERICAN
Skinless cod fillet	100 g	4 oz	4 oz
Milk	300 ml	½ pint	1¼ cups
Sweet potato	75 g	3 oz	3 oz
Canned or frozen sweetcorn (corn)	50 g	2 oz	2 oz
Fresh sprig of parsley, stalk removed (optional)	1	1	1

① Put the fish in a small pan with the milk. Slowly bring to a simmer and poach for 7–8 minutes or until the fish is cooked. Remove the fish from the pan, using a slotted spoon, flake into pieces, taking care to remove any bones, and set aside. Reserve the milk.

② Meanwhile, peel the sweet potato and cut into 2.5 cm/1 in dice. Add to the milk. Bring to the boil and simmer for 10 minutes. Add the sweetcorn and parsley and cook for a further 5 minutes or until the sweet potato is very tender.

③ Purée the vegetable and milk mixture with the fish until fairly smooth. Spoon a portion into a bowl and allow to cool slightly, if necessary, before serving.

④ Cool the remaining purée, divide into portions and freeze, or cover and store in the fridge for up to 24 hours.

CHICKEN WITH GARDEN VEGETABLES

MAKES 6 BABY PORTIONS

❋	METRIC	IMPERIAL	AMERICAN
Small carrot	1	1	1
Potato	100 g	4 oz	4 oz
Green (French) beans	4	4	4
Chicken breast, skinned and boned	100 g	4 oz	4 oz
Milk	150 ml	¼ pint	⅔ cup

①   Trim and peel the carrot and potato and cut into small cubes. Trim the beans and cut each into 3 or 4 pieces. Slice the chicken into thin strips. Put in a small saucepan with the vegetables and add the milk.

②   Part-cover the pan with a lid and simmer for 15 minutes or until the chicken and vegetables are cooked.

③   Purée the mixture until fairly smooth. Spoon a portion into a bowl and allow to cool, if necessary, before serving.

④   Cool the remaining purée, divide into portions and freeze, or cover and store in the fridge for up to 24 hours.

ONE-POT CHICKEN AND RICE

MAKES 6 BABY PORTIONS

❄	METRIC	IMPERIAL	AMERICAN
Long-grain rice	50 g	2 oz	¼ cup
Milk	300 ml	½ pint	1 ¼ cups
Chicken breast, skinned and boned	100 g	4 oz	4 oz
Small carrot	1	1	1
Broccoli	100 g	4 oz	4 oz

① Rinse the rice under cold running water and put in a small saucepan with the milk.

② Cut the chicken into thin strips. Trim, peel and slice the carrot. Divide the broccoli into small florets. Add to the pan and bring to the boil.

③ Stir, then part-cover the pan with a lid and simmer for 12–15 minutes or until the rice and vegetables are soft.

④ Purée the mixture until fairly smooth. Spoon a portion into a bowl and allow to cool slightly, if necessary, before serving.

⑤ Cool the remaining purée, divide into portions and freeze, or cover and store in the fridge for up to 24 hours.

BROCCOLI AND CAULIFLOWER CHEESE

Serve this vegetable dish as part the family meal. Remember to remove a couple of portions for baby before seasoning.

MAKES 2 ADULT PLUS 2 BABY PORTIONS

❄	METRIC	IMPERIAL	AMERICAN
Medium cauliflower, cut into florets	½	½	½
Broccoli, cut into florets	225 g	8 oz	8 oz
Butter or margarine	40 g	1½ oz	scant ¼ cup
Plain (all-purpose) flour	45 ml	3 tbsp	3 tbsp
Bay leaf	1	1	1
Milk	300 ml	½ pint	1¼ cups
Mild or medium Cheddar cheese, grated	75 g	3 oz	¾ cup

1. Add the cauliflower and broccoli florets to a pan of boiling water, cover and simmer for 10 minutes or until tender. Alternatively, put in a steamer over boiling water and cook for 12 minutes.

2. Meanwhile, put the butter or margarine, flour, bay leaf and milk in a small saucepan. Slowly bring to the boil, stirring all the time until the sauce thickens. Turn down the heat and simmer for 3 minutes. Discard the bay leaf.

3. Remove the sauce from the heat and stir in the grated cheese until melted. Remove three florets each of cauliflower and broccoli and about 60 ml/4 tbsp of the sauce. (The remainder will serve two adults.) Mash together with a fork or purée until fairly smooth, adding a little extra milk if needed.

4. Spoon half the purée into a bowl and allow to cool slightly, if necessary, before serving. Cool the remaining portion and freeze or cover and store in the fridge for up to 24 hours.

Tip: If you prefer, make half the quantity of this recipe and divide into six portions for baby meals.

BEEF AND CARROT BRAISE

MAKES 6 BABY PORTIONS

✾	METRIC	IMPERIAL	AMERICAN
Lean stewing beef	100 g	4 oz	4 oz
Sunflower oil	15 ml	1 tbsp	1 tbsp
Spring onions (scallions)	4	4	4
Medium carrot	1	1	1
Potato	175 g	6 oz	6 oz
Yeast extract, such as Marmite	1.5 ml	¼ tsp	¼ tsp
A pinch of dried mixed herbs			
Hot vegetable stock (page 38) or water	300 ml	½ pint	1¼ cups

① Trim any fat or gristle from the beef and cut the meat into small cubes. Heat the oil in a small flameproof casserole dish (Dutch oven), add the beef and fry (sauté) until lightly browned. Remove from the heat.

② Trim the spring onions and cut them into 2.5 cm/1 in lengths. Trim and peel the carrot and potato. Cut the vegetables into large cubes and add to the casserole dish.

③ Stir the yeast extract and herbs into the hot vegetable stock or water and pour over the meat and vegetables.

④ Cover the casserole and simmer very gently for about 1 hour or until the meat is tender. Alternatively, cook in a preheated oven at 180°C/350°F/gas mark 4 for 1½ hours.

⑤ Purée the mixture until fairly smooth. Spoon a portion into a bowl and allow to cool slightly, if necessary, before serving.

⑥ Cool the remaining purée, divide into portions and freeze, or cover and store in the fridge for up to 24 hours.

Tip: Yeast extract is very salty so don't be tempted to add more than the recipe states.

SAVOURY PORK AND APPLE CASSEROLE

MAKES 6 BABY PORTIONS

	METRIC	IMPERIAL	AMERICAN
Lean pork, such as tenderloin	100 g	4 oz	4 oz
Potato	100 g	4 oz	4 oz
Parsnip	100 g	4 oz	4 oz
Small eating (dessert) apple	1	1	1
A pinch of dried mixed herbs			
Vegetable stock (page 38) or water	300 ml	½ pint	1¼ cups

① Trim any fat or gristle from the pork and slice thinly. Peel the potato and parsnip and cut into chunks. Peel, quarter and core the apple and roughly chop.

② Put the meat, vegetables, apple, herbs and stock or water in a small pan. Bring to the boil, cover and simmer gently for about 45 minutes or until the meat is tender. Alternatively, cook in a preheated oven at 180°C/350°F/gas mark 4 for 1¼ hours.

③ Purée the mixture until fairly smooth. Spoon a portion into a bowl and allow to cool slightly, if necessary, before serving.

④ Cool the remaining purée, divide into portions and freeze, or cover and store in the fridge for up to 24 hours.

Tip: The parsnip can be replaced with another root vegetable such as swede (rutabaga) or carrot.

POACHED FISH WITH PEA AND POTATO PURÉE

MAKES 4 BABY PORTIONS

❄	METRIC	IMPERIAL	AMERICAN
Plaice fillet, skinned	100 g	4 oz	4 oz
Bay leaf	1	1	1
Milk	150 ml	¼ pint	⅔ cup
Potato	100 g	4 oz	4 oz
Frozen peas	25 g	1 oz	1 oz
Snipped fresh chives or chopped fresh parsley (optional)	5 ml	1 tsp	1 tsp

① Put the fish in a small saucepan with the bay leaf. Pour over the milk. Slowly bring to the boil, part-cover the pan with a lid and simmer for 10–12 minutes or until the fish is cooked.

② Remove the fish from the milk using a slotted spoon, then flake the flesh and roughly mash with a fork, removing any bones. Discard the bay leaf and reserve the milk.

③ Meanwhile, peel the potato and cut into chunks. Cook in boiling water for 10 minutes. Add the peas and cook for a further 5 minutes or until the potato is tender. Drain well.

④ Mash the potato and peas with enough of the reserved milk to make a smooth mixture. Stir in the fish and herbs, if using.

⑤ Spoon a portion into a bowl and allow to cool slightly, if necessary, before serving.

⑥ Cool the remaining purée, divide into portions and freeze, or cover and store in the fridge for up to 24 hours.

CREAM OF CARROT AND COURGETTE

MAKES 2 BABY PORTIONS

	METRIC	IMPERIAL	AMERICAN
Medium carrot	I	I	I
Small courgette (zucchini)	½	½	½
Warm milk	75 ml	5 tbsp	5 tbsp
Baby rice	15 ml	I tbsp	I tbsp

① Trim, peel and slice the carrot. Wash, trim and slice the courgette. Put in a steamer or a sieve (strainer), placed over a pan of boiling water, and cook for about 15 minutes or until very soft.

② Purée the vegetables with 60 ml/4 tbsp of the milk until fairly smooth.

③ Blend the rice and remaining milk together, then stir in the puréed vegetables.

④ Spoon half the purée into a bowl and allow to cool slightly, if necessary, before serving.

⑤ Cool the remaining purée, cover and store in the fridge for up to 24 hours.

CREAMY CARROT AND CORIANDER WITH LENTILS

MAKES 4 BABY PORTIONS

✱	METRIC	IMPERIAL	AMERICAN
Medium carrots	3	3	3
Red lentils	50 g	2 oz	¼ cup
Milk	200 ml	7 fl oz	scant 1 cup
Chopped fresh coriander (cilantro)	2.5 ml	½ tsp	½ tsp

① Trim, peel and slice the carrots and put in a small saucepan. Rinse and pick over the lentils. Add to the pan with the milk.

② Bring to the boil, turn down the heat, cover and simmer for about 30 minutes or until the lentils are very soft. Stir in the coriander.

③ Sieve (strain) or purée the mixture until fairly smooth. Spoon a portion into a bowl and allow to cool slightly, if necessary, before serving.

④ Cool the remaining purée, divide into portions and freeze, or cover and store in the fridge for up to 24 hours.

Tip: You can use fresh parsley instead of the coriander, or leave it out altogether if preferred.

CREAMED POTATO AND CELERIAC WITH CHEESE

You can also turn this vegetable purée into a delicious dish for two or three adults to accompany chicken or game by seasoning with salt, black pepper and plenty of freshly grated nutmeg after removing a portion for baby.

MAKES 4 BABY PORTIONS

❊ (SEE TIP)	METRIC	IMPERIAL	AMERICAN
Potato	175 g	6 oz	6 oz
Celeriac (celery root)	175 g	6 oz	6 oz
Butter or margarine	25 g	1 oz	2 tbsp
Milk	75 ml	5 tbsp	5 tbsp
Mild Cheddar cheese, finely grated	15 g	½ oz	1 tbsp

① Peel the potato and celeriac and cut into large chunks. Cook in boiling water for 15 minutes or until very tender. Drain well.

② Mash the vegetables together with the butter or margarine and milk until smooth, adding a little more milk if needed.

③ Spoon a portion into a bowl. Allow to cool slightly, if necessary, stir in the cheese, then serve.

④ Cool the remaining purée, divide into portions and freeze, or cover and store in the fridge for up to 24 hours.

Tip: Don't add the cheese before freezing the vegetable purée, as it tends to go stringy when reheated.

QUICK FISH KEDGEREE

MAKES 6 BABY PORTIONS

	METRIC	IMPERIAL	AMERICAN
Long-grain rice	50 g	2 oz	¼ cup
Frozen skinless cod fillet	100 g	4 oz	4 oz
Milk	300 ml	½ pint	1¼ cups
Hard-boiled (hard-cooked) egg yolk	1	1	1
Chopped fresh parsley	10 ml	2 tsp	2 tsp

① Rinse the rice under cold running water. Put it in a small saucepan with the cod and milk. Bring to the boil, part-cover the pan with a lid and simmer for 15 minutes or until the rice and fish are cooked.

② Remove the fish from the pan and flake with a fork, removing any bones. Stir the fish into the rice with the egg yolk and parsley. Mash or purée the mixture until fairly smooth.

③ Spoon a portion into a bowl and allow to cool slightly, if necessary, before serving.

④ Cool the remaining mixture, divide into portions and freeze, or cover and store in the fridge for up to 24 hours.

LEEK AND POTATO PURÉE

To turn this into a tasty soup for 3–4 adults, double the quantity, season and thin down with extra stock or milk and serve topped with crème fraîche and a sprinkling of snipped fresh chives.

MAKES 6 BABY PORTIONS

❀ (SEE TIP)	METRIC	IMPERIAL	AMERICAN
Small or baby leeks	175 g	6 oz	6 oz
Butter or margarine	25 g	1 oz	2 tbsp
Floury potatoes	100 g	4 oz	4 oz
Bay leaf	1	1	1
Vegetable stock (page 38)	120 ml	4 fl oz	½ cup
Milk	120 ml	4 fl oz	½ cup
Plain fromage frais, to serve			

①   Trim and thoroughly wash the leeks. Cut into thin slices.

②   Melt the butter or margarine in a saucepan. Add the leeks and cook over a gentle heat for 10 minutes, until soft.

③   Meanwhile, peel the potatoes and cut into chunks. Add the potato chunks to the leeks with the bay leaf, stock and milk. Bring to the boil, lower the heat, cover and simmer for 20 minutes until the potatoes are tender.

④   Discard the bay leaf. Purée the vegetable mixture until fairly smooth. Spoon a portion into a bowl and allow to cool slightly if necessary. Stir 30 ml/2 tbsp of fromage frais before serving.

⑤   Cool the remaining purée, divide into portions and freeze, or cover and store in the fridge for up to 24 hours.

Tips: Freeze without the fromage frais. Use all milk instead of a mixture of stock and milk, if preferred.

POTATO AND WATERCRESS PURÉE WITH FROMAGE FRAIS

MAKES 2 BABY PORTIONS

	METRIC	IMPERIAL	AMERICAN
Potato	100 g	4 oz	4 oz
Sprigs of watercress	2–3	2–3	2–3
Butter or margarine	15 g	½ oz	2 tbsp
Plain fromage frais	60 ml	4 tbsp	4 tbsp

① Peel the potato and cut it into chunks. Cook in boiling salted water for 15 minutes or until tender. Drain well.

② Meanwhile, remove the tough stems from the watercress and finely chop the leaves. Melt the butter or margarine in a small pan and gently cook the watercress for about 2 minutes until wilted and tender.

③ Mash the potato with the watercress, butter or margarine and fromage frais until smooth. Spoon half into a bowl and allow to cool slightly, if necessary, before serving.

④ Cool the remaining mixture, cover and store in the fridge for up to 24 hours.

MEDITERRANEAN VEGETABLES WITH PASTA

MAKES 6 BABY PORTIONS

❋	METRIC	IMPERIAL	AMERICAN
Ripe tomatoes	2	2	2
Small courgette (zucchini)	I	I	I
Red (bell) pepper	100 g	4 oz	4 oz
Tomato purée (paste)	5 ml	I tsp	I tsp
Vegetable stock (page 38) or water	175 ml	6 fl oz	¾ cup
A small pinch of dried basil or dried mixed herbs			
Mini pasta shapes	25 g	I oz	I oz

①   Plunge the tomatoes into boiling water for 1 minute, then remove, rinse under cold water and peel off the skins, then quarter and remove the seeds.

②   Rinse, trim and slice the courgette. Cut away the core and seeds from the pepper, then chop. Put the vegetables in a saucepan with the tomato purée, stock or water and herbs. Cover and simmer for 10 minutes.

③   Add the pasta and cook for a further 5 minutes or until the vegetables and pasta are very soft.

④   Purée or mash the mixture with a fork until fairly smooth. Spoon a portion into a bowl and allow to cool slightly, if necessary, before serving.

⑤   Cool the remaining purée, divide into portions and freeze, or cover and store in the fridge for up to 24 hours.

Tip: Soup pastas such as stellette or anellini are an ideal choice for this recipe.

VEGETABLE MEDLEY

MAKES 6 BABY PORTIONS

	METRIC	IMPERIAL	AMERICAN
Swede (rutabaga)	100 g	4 oz	4 oz
Potato	100 g	4 oz	4 oz
Broccoli	100 g	4 oz	4 oz
Green cabbage	50 g	2 oz	2 oz
Milk	250 ml	8 fl oz	1 cup

① Peel and dice the swede and potato. Cut the broccoli into florets and finely shred the cabbage. Put the vegetables in a small saucepan with the milk.

② Bring to the boil, lower the heat and cook, part-covered, for 12–15 minutes until all the vegetables are very tender.

③ Sieve (strain) or purée the mixture until fairly smooth. Spoon a portion into a bowl and allow to cool slightly, if necessary, before serving.

④ Cool the remaining purée, divide into portions and freeze, or cover and store in the fridge for up to 24 hours.

CHOCOLATE RICE PUDDING

MAKES 2 BABY PORTIONS

	METRIC	IMPERIAL	AMERICAN
Flaked rice	30 ml	2 tbsp	2 tbsp
Milk	150 ml	¼ pint	⅔ cup
Milk chocolate	25 g	1 oz	1 oz

① Place the flaked rice and milk in a small saucepan. Bring to the boil and simmer over a gentle heat for 10 minutes, until the rice is cooked, stirring occasionally. Remove from the heat.

② Roughly chop the chocolate and add to the hot rice. Stir until melted. Spoon half into a bowl and allow to cool slightly, if necessary, before serving.

③ Cool the remaining portion, cover and store in the fridge for up to 24 hours.

BAKED SWEET POTATO AND APPLE

MAKES 6 BABY PORTIONS

	METRIC	IMPERIAL	AMERICAN
Medium sweet potato	I	I	I
Eating (dessert) apple	I	I	I
Butter or margarine	15 g	½ oz	I tbsp
Milk	45 ml	3 tbsp	3 tbsp
A small pinch of ground cinnamon			

① Gently scrub the sweet potato. Cut a thin slice from the base of the apple so that it stands upright.

② Prick the sweet potato and apple several times with a fork or skewer, place in an ovenproof dish and loosely cover with foil. Bake in a preheated oven at 180°C/350°F/gas mark 4 for 40–50 minutes or until tender. Leave until cool enough to handle.

③ Halve the sweet potato and scoop out the flesh. Mash with the butter or margarine, milk and cinnamon until smooth.

④ Halve the apple and remove the core and pips. Scoop out the flesh and add to the potato. Mash until mixed together.

⑤ Spoon a portion into a bowl and allow to cool slightly, if necessary, before serving.

⑥ Cool the remaining purée and freeze, or cover and store in the fridge for up to 24 hours.

APPLE AND RASPBERRY RIPPLE YOGHURT

MAKES 4 BABY PORTIONS

✿ (SEE TIP)	METRIC	IMPERIAL	AMERICAN
Eating (dessert) apple	I	I	I
Apple juice or water	I5 ml	I tbsp	I tbsp
Fresh or frozen raspberries	25 g	I oz	I oz
Plain Greek yoghurt, to serve			

① Peel, quarter and core the apple, then slice it thinly. Put it in a small saucepan with the apple juice or water, cover and simmer gently for 5 minutes. Add the raspberries and cook for a further 5 minutes or until very soft.

② Mash the fruit with a fork, then press though a fine sieve (strainer) to remove the berry pips. Leave the purée to cool.

③ Spoon a quarter of the purée into a bowl. Divide the rest into portions and freeze or cover and store in the fridge for up to 24 hours.

④ Add 10 ml/2 tsp of yoghurt to the portion of fruit purée and stir to achieve a rippled effect. Serve straight away.

Tip: Freeze without the yoghurt.

PEAR AND PRUNE CUSTARD

MAKES 6 BABY PORTIONS

❋	METRIC	IMPERIAL	AMERICAN
Prunes	2	2	2
Apple juice or water	75 ml	5 tbsp	5 tbsp
Ripe pear	I	I	I
Custard powder	15 ml	I tbsp	I tbsp
Caster (superfine) sugar	5 ml	I tsp	I tsp
Milk	150 ml	¼ pint	⅔ cup

① Halve and stone (pit) the prunes. Put them in a small bowl with the apple juice or water and leave to soak for at least 4 hours or overnight.

② Peel, quarter, core and slice the pear. Put it in a small saucepan with the prunes and soaking liquid. Cover and simmer for 10 minutes until soft, stirring occasionally. Rub the fruit through a sieve (strainer) to remove the tough prune skins.

③ Meanwhile, blend the custard powder with the sugar and 30 ml/2 tbsp of the milk. Heat the remaining milk in a pan until boiling, then pour over the custard and milk paste, stirring. Return to the pan and simmer for 1 minute, stirring continuously, until thickened and smooth.

④ Stir the fruit purée into the custard. Spoon a portion into a bowl and allow to cool slightly, if necessary, before serving.

⑤ Cool the remaining custard, divide into portions and freeze, or cover and store in the fridge for up to 24 hours.

BLUSHING PEAR DESSERT

Strawberries or raspberries work equally well in this recipe.

MAKES 4 BABY PORTIONS

❋ (SEE TIP)	METRIC	IMPERIAL	AMERICAN
Ripe pear	I	I	I
Fresh or frozen blackberries	25 g	I oz	I oz
Orange juice	15 ml	I tbsp	I tbsp
Fromage frais, to serve			

① Quarter, core and peel the pear. Slice thinly and put in a small saucepan with the blackberries and orange juice. Cover and simmer for 10 minutes until very soft. Press the mixture through a sieve (strainer) to remove the berry pips.

② Spoon a quarter of the purée into a bowl. When cool, stir in 10 ml/2 tsp of fromage frais and serve straight away.

③ Cool the remaining fruit purée, divide into portions and freeze, or cover and store in the fridge for up to 24 hours.

Tip: Freeze without the fromage frais.

BANANA CREAM

MAKES I PORTION

❋	METRIC	IMPERIAL	AMERICAN
Ripe banana	½	½	½
Silken tofu	40 g	I ½ oz	I ½ oz
Orange juice	30 ml	2 tbsp	2 tbsp

① Peel and roughly chop the banana. Put in a food processor with the tofu and orange juice and blend to a smooth purée.

② Spoon into a bowl and serve straight away, or cover and chill in the fridge for up to 4 hours.

ORCHARD FRUIT FOOL

MAKES 6 BABY PORTIONS

	METRIC	IMPERIAL	AMERICAN
Eating (dessert) apple	1	1	1
Ripe plums	2	2	2
Apple or orange juice	15 ml	1 tbsp	1 tbsp
Custard powder	15 ml	1 tbsp	1 tbsp
Soft light brown sugar	10 ml	2 tsp	2 tsp
Milk	150 ml	¼ pint	⅔ cup

① Quarter, core and peel the apple. Half the plums, remove the stones (pits) and peel off the skins. Roughly chop the fruit and put in a small saucepan with the apple or orange juice.

② Cover and simmer for 10 minutes or until the fruit is very tender. Mash the fruit with a fork until fairly smooth.

③ Meanwhile, blend the custard powder with the sugar and 30 ml/2 tbsp of the milk until smooth. Heat the remaining milk to boiling point and pour over the custard and milk paste, stirring.

④ Return the custard to the pan and simmer, stirring for 1 minute, until thickened and smooth. Stir in the fruit purée.

⑤ Spoon a portion into a bowl and allow to cool slightly, if necessary, before serving.

⑥ Cool the remaining mixture, divide into portions and freeze, or cover and store in the fridge for up to 24 hours.

BAKED EGG CUSTARD

Babies shouldn't be given egg whites until they're at least nine months old, so this custard is made with just the yolk.

MAKES 2 BABY PORTIONS

✦	METRIC	IMPERIAL	AMERICAN
Egg yolk	1	1	1
Cornflour (cornstarch)	2.5 ml	½ tsp	½ tsp
Caster (superfine) sugar	5 ml	1 tsp	1 tsp
A few drops of vanilla essence (extract)			
Milk	175 ml	6 fl oz	scant 1 cup

①   Blend the egg yolk with the cornflour, sugar and vanilla essence in a bowl. Heat the milk to boiling point, then pour over the egg mixture, whisking all the time.

②   Pour the mixture into two small greased ramekins (custard cups), placed in a roasting tin (pan) or ovenproof dish. Pour enough water into the tin to come halfway up the sides of the ramekins and cover each with a small piece of foil.

③   Bake in a preheated oven at 150°C/300°F/gas mark 2 for 35 minutes or until lightly set. Serve one portion warm or cold.

④   Allow the remaining portion to cool. Cover and chill in the fridge for up to 24 hours.

⑤   Serve cold. Do not reheat.

TEETHING RUSKS

Most commercial baby rusks contain a large amount of sugar, which can decay teeth as they start to come through. Try these savoury toasts as a simple and inexpensive alternative.

MAKES 8

	METRIC	IMPERIAL	AMERICAN
Yeast extract	1.5 ml	¼ tsp	¼ tsp
Boiling water	15 ml	1 tbsp	1 tbsp
Slices of white bread	2	2	2

① Mix together the yeast extract and water until blended. Very lightly brush the mixture over one side of each slice of bread.

② Trim the crusts off the bread and cut each slice into four fingers. Bake in a preheated oven at 160°C/325°F/gas mark 3 for 25 minutes or until crisp and dry.

③ Leave to cool on a wire rack. Transfer to an airtight container and store for up to 5 days.

NINE TO TWELVE MONTHS

Your baby will now be eating slightly more textured meals, and by the time she is one year old her food should be roughly mashed or very finely chopped. Give her three main meals a day, plus two or three healthy snacks between meals, such as a few finger foods or a small pot of fromage frais. At this age, children need to eat little and often as they are growing rapidly. This shouldn't affect their appetite at meal times, but obviously don't give snacks just before main meals and try not to give too many sweet sugary snacks such as biscuits (cookies). Keep added sugar and sugary foods to a minimum

You should still avoid seasoning food with salt, but you can start to use flavourings containing some salt, such as good-quality stock cubes. Some of the recipes here call for vegetable stock. You can use either the salt-free recipe on page 38 or commercial stock cubes or granules.

FINGER FOODS

These not only provide useful nutrients, but also aid your baby's co-ordination and help her on the way to self-feeding. Try to serve a selection, mixing high protein and carbohydrate foods with fresh fruit and vegetables. When she's teething, chewing and sucking will soothe sore gums and chilling sticks of raw fruit and vegetables before serving may help.

SIMPLE IDEAS FOR FINGER FOODS

◇ Bread sticks, rusks, fingers of white or wholemeal (but not wholegrain) toast

◇ Cooked pasta shapes

◇ Cubes of cooked chicken

◇ Cubes of mild cheese, such as Cheddar or Edam

◇ Mini sandwiches

◇ Pieces of dried sugar-free breakfast cereal (but not high-fibre varieties)

◇ Quartered, peeled and cored ripe pear or apple, peeled firm but ripe banana

◇ Sticks of carrot or celery, cut into easy-to-hold pieces

FOODS TO AVOID AT NINE TO TWELVE MONTHS

◇ Honey

◇ Salt; but you can now use small amounts of stock, yeast extracts and similar flavourings

◇ Shellfish

◇ Nuts, including peanut butter and sesame seeds

CHUNKY BEEF CASSEROLE

MAKES 2 ADULT PLUS 2 BABY PORTIONS

❋	METRIC	IMPERIAL	AMERICAN
Braising steak	350 g	12 oz	12 oz
Sunflower oil	30 ml	2 tbsp	2 tbsp
Garlic clove, crushed	1	1	1
Large onion, chopped	1	1	1
Plain (all-purpose) flour	30 ml	2 tbsp	2 tbsp
Beef stock	600 ml	1 pint	2½ cups
Soft light brown sugar	5 ml	1 tsp	1 tsp
Dried mixed herbs	2.5 ml	½ tsp	½ tsp
Worcestershire sauce	10 ml	2 tsp	2 tsp
Tomato purée (paste)	15 ml	1 tbsp	1 tbsp
Bay leaf	1	1	1
Celery sticks, sliced	2	2	2
Medium carrots, sliced	2	2	2
Potatoes, peeled and cut into chunks	450 g	1 lb	1 lb
Salt and freshly ground black pepper			

① Trim any fat from the beef and cut the meat into small cubes.

② Heat 15 ml/1 tbsp of the oil in an ovenproof casserole dish (Dutch oven) and lightly fry (sauté) the beef until well browned. Remove from the pan with a slotted spoon and set aside.

③ Heat the remaining oil in the casserole and gently fry the garlic and onion for 10 minutes. Sprinkle over the flour and stir in. Gradually stir in the stock, then the sugar, herbs, Worcestershire sauce, tomato purée and bay leaf. Add the celery and carrots.

④ Slowly bring to the boil, stirring until thickened. Cover and cook in a preheated oven at 160°C/325°F/gas mark 3 for 1½ hours.

⑤ Add the potatoes and cook for a further 30–40 minutes or until the meat and potatoes are tender.

⑥ Remove two baby portions. Season the remainder to be served as adult portions.

⑦ Chop the meat and vegetables for the baby portions, or purée until the desired consistency. Spoon half into a bowl and allow to cool slightly, if necessary, before serving.

⑧ Cool the remaining portion, cover and freeze or store in the fridge for up to 24 hours.

Tip: If preferred, cook half the recipe quantity, purée to the desired consistency and divide into 10 baby-sized portions before freezing.

BEEFY BEAN DINNER

MAKES 4 BABY PORTIONS

❄	METRIC	IMPERIAL	AMERICAN
Sunflower oil	15 ml	I tbsp	I tbsp
Small onion, finely chopped	I	I	I
Lean minced (ground) beef	100 g	4 oz	4 oz
Macaroni	50 g	2 oz	2 oz
Beef or vegetable stock (page 38)	250 ml	8 fl oz	I cup
Tomato juice	100 ml	3½ fl oz	scant ½ cup
Baked beans	50 g	2 oz	2 oz

① Heat the oil in a saucepan and gently fry (sauté) the onion for 5 minutes, until beginning to soften. Add the minced beef and cook for a further 5 minutes until the meat is lightly browned.

② Add the macaroni, stock and tomato juice. Stir once, cover and simmer for 15 minutes. Stir in the baked beans and cook for a further 5 minutes or until the pasta is tender.

③ Lightly chop or purée the mixture to the desired consistency. Spoon a portion into a bowl and allow to cool slightly, if necessary, before serving.

④ Cool the remaining mixture, divide into portions and freeze, or cover and store in the fridge for up to 24 hours.

SHEPHERDS' PIE

MAKES 2–3 ADULT PLUS 2 BABY PORTIONS

❋

	METRIC	IMPERIAL	AMERICAN
Lean minced (ground) lamb	350 g	12 oz	12 oz
Medium onion, finely chopped	1	1	1
Mushrooms, finely chopped	50 g	2 oz	2 oz
Carrots, finely diced	2	2	2
Plain (all-purpose) flour	30 ml	2 tbsp	2 tbsp
Lamb or vegetable stock (page 38)	300 ml	½ pint	1¼ cups
Tomato purée (paste)	15 ml	1 tbsp	1 tbsp
Bay leaf	1	1	1
Potatoes, cut into chunks	700 g	1½ lb	1½ lb
Butter or margarine	25 g	1 oz	2 tbsp
Milk	75 ml	5 tbsp	5 tbsp
Salt and freshly ground black pepper			

① Fry (sauté) the minced lamb in a non-stick saucepan for 4–5 minutes or until browned. Using a slotted spoon, transfer the meat to a plate, leaving the juices in the pan. Add the onion to the pan and gently cook for 10 minutes, until softened and beginning to brown.

② Add the mushrooms and carrots to the pan and fry for a further 2 minutes. Sprinkle over the flour and stir in. Gradually stir in the stock and tomato purée. Return the meat to the pan, add the bay leaf and cook, stirring, until the mixture thickens and boils. Cover and simmer gently for 30 minutes.

③ Remove the bay leaf and spoon enough mixture to half-fill two 150 ml/¼ pint/⅔ cup ovenproof dishes. Season the remaining mixture with salt and pepper and spoon into a large ovenproof dish.

④ Meanwhile, cook the potatoes in boiling water for about 20 minutes until tender. Drain and mash with the butter or margarine and milk until smooth. Spoon a little over the meat mixture in the two small dishes. Season the remaining potato with salt and pepper and pile on to the meat mixture in the large dish.

⑤ Bake the pies in a preheated oven at 190°C/375°F/gas mark 5, allowing 15 minutes for the small pies and 25 minutes for the larger one, until lightly browned.

⑥ Leave one of the baby portions to cool slightly before serving – this is quicker if you spoon it into a bowl. Cool the remaining portion completely. Cover and freeze or store in the fridge for up to 24 hours.

Tip: If preferred, make up half the recipe quantity and use it to make eight baby portions.

COUNTRY PORK WITH BROCCOLI

MAKES 4 BABY PORTIONS

❁	METRIC	IMPERIAL	AMERICAN
Lean pork, such as fillet	100 g	4 oz	4 oz
Potato, roughly chopped	100 g	4 oz	4 oz
Medium carrot, roughly chopped	1	1	1
Vegetable stock (page 38) or water	300 ml	½ pint	1¼ cups
Broccoli	100 g	4 oz	4 oz
Milk	60 ml	4 tbsp	4 tbsp

① Trim any fat from the pork and cut the meat into small cubes. Put the potato and carrot into a small saucepan with the stock or water. Bring to the boil, cover and simmer gently for 25 minutes.

② Cut the broccoli into florets, add to the pan and cook for a further 10 minutes or until the meat and vegetables are tender. Remove from the heat, cool for a few minutes, then stir in the milk.

③ Purée the mixture to the desired consistency. Spoon a portion into a bowl and allow to cool slightly, if necessary, before serving.

④ Cool the remaining mixture, divide into portions and freeze, or cover and store in the fridge for up to 24 hours.

PAPRIKA PORK WITH RICE AND BEANS

MAKES 4 BABY PORTIONS

❃	METRIC	IMPERIAL	AMERICAN
Lean pork, such as fillet	100 g	4 oz	4 oz
Sunflower oil	10 ml	2 tsp	2 tsp
Long-grain rice	50 g	2 oz	¼ cup
Paprika	1.5 ml	¼ tsp	¼ tsp
Milk	300 ml	½ pint	1¼ cups
Baked beans in tomato sauce	75 g	3 oz	½ cup

① Cut the pork into 5 mm/¼ in cubes. Heat the oil in a non-stick saucepan and cook the pork until lightly browned. Stir in the rice and paprika, then pour in the milk. Bring to the boil and simmer, uncovered, for 12 minutes.

② Stir in the beans, lower the heat, cover and cook for a further 2–3 minutes or until the pork and rice are tender. Lightly mash or purée to the desired consistency.

③ Spoon a portion into a bowl and allow to cool slightly, if necessary, before serving.

④ Cool the remainder, divide into portions and freeze or cover and store in the fridge for up to 24 hours.

BACON AND BEAN FEAST

MAKES 4 BABY PORTIONS

❄	METRIC	IMPERIAL	AMERICAN
Rasher (slice) of unsmoked back bacon	I	I	I
Potatoes, cut into chunks	225 g	8 oz	8 oz
Butter or margarine	15 g	½ oz	I tbsp
Milk	30 ml	2 tbsp	2 tbsp
Mild Cheddar cheese, finely grated	25 g	I oz	¼ cup
Can of baked beans in tomato sauce	200 g	7 oz	I small

① Remove the fat and rind from the bacon. Chop the bacon into tiny pieces and dry-fry in a non-stick pan for 2–3 minutes until cooked.

② Cook the potatoes in boiling water for 20 minutes or until tender. Drain well and mash with the butter or margarine, milk and cheese.

③ Lightly mash the beans with a fork, then add to the bacon and stir to mix. Divide the mixture between four 150 ml/ ¼ pint/⅔ cup ovenproof dishes and spoon the mashed potato on top.

④ Bake one of the portions in a preheated oven at 190°C/ 375°F/gas mark 5 for 20 minutes or until the top is golden brown. Alternatively, microwave on High for 5 minutes, then brown the top under a grill (broiler) for 1 minute, if liked. Leave to cool to the desired serving temperature.

⑤ Cover and freeze the remaining portions, or store in the fridge for up to 24 hours.

FRUITY LAMB COUSCOUS

MAKES 4 BABY PORTIONS

❄	METRIC	IMPERIAL	AMERICAN
Mixed dried fruit, such as apple rings, apricots and prunes	50 g	2 oz	⅓ cup
Lamb or vegetable stock (page 38)	300 ml	½ pint	1¼ cups
Lean lamb, such as fillet	175 g	6 oz	6 oz
Medium carrot, finely chopped	1	1	1
Sunflower oil	10 ml	2 tsp	2 tsp
Tomato purée (paste)	5 ml	1 tsp	1 tsp
Couscous	50 g	2 oz	⅓ cup

① Rinse the fruit under cold running water to remove any preservative. Chop finely and put in a bowl. Pour over the stock or water and leave to soak for at least 1 hour.

② Trim any fat from the lamb and cut it into small cubes. Heat the oil in a saucepan and fry (sauté) the lamb until browned. Add the carrot and cook for 1 minute, stirring all the time.

③ Stir in the fruit with the stock or water and tomato purée. Cover and simmer gently for 30 minutes or until the lamb is almost tender.

④ Put the couscous in a sieve (strainer) and rinse under cold running water. Place the sieve over the lamb in the pan, cover and steam for 20 minutes.

⑤ Chop or process the lamb and vegetable mixture to the desired consistency. Stir in the steamed couscous.

⑥ Spoon a portion into a bowl and allow to cool slightly, if necessary, before serving.

⑦ Cool the remainder, divide into portions and freeze, or cover and store in the fridge for up to 24 hours.

LAMB AND LENTIL SUPPER

MAKES 4 BABY PORTIONS

	METRIC	IMPERIAL	AMERICAN
Lean lamb, such as fillet	100 g	4 oz	4 oz
Red lentils	25 g	1 oz	2 tbsp
Sweet potato, cut into chunks	100 g	4 oz	4 oz
Tomato purée (paste)	5 ml	1 tsp	1 tsp
Lamb or vegetable stock (page 38)	350 ml	12 fl oz	1½ cups

① Trim any fat from the lamb and cut it into small cubes. Put the lentils in a sieve (strainer) and rinse under cold water.

② Put all the ingredients in a small saucepan. Slowly bring to the boil, cover and simmer gently for 35 minutes or until the lamb and lentils are tender. Check towards the end of cooking time and add a little more stock or water if needed.

③ Mash or purée the mixture to the desired consistency. Spoon a portion into a bowl and allow to cool slightly, if necessary, before serving.

④ Cool the remaining mixture, divide into portions and freeze, or cover and store in the fridge for up to 24 hours.

TURKEY AND TOMATO HOTPOT

MAKES 4 BABY PORTIONS

	METRIC	IMPERIAL	AMERICAN
Turkey breast, skinned and boned	100 g	4 oz	4 oz
Long-grain rice	50 g	2 oz	¼ cup
Chicken or turkey stock	150 ml	¼ pint	⅔ cup
Tomato juice	150 ml	¼ pint	⅔ cup
Frozen peas	25 g	1 oz	1 oz

① Cut the turkey into thin strips. Put in a small saucepan with all the remaining ingredients. Bring to the boil, cover and simmer for 15 minutes or until the turkey and rice are cooked.

② Purée the mixture to the desired consistency. Spoon a portion into a bowl and allow to cool slightly, if necessary, before serving.

③ Cool the remaining mixture, divide into portions and freeze, or cover and store in the fridge for up to 24 hours.

CHICKEN AND VEGETABLE BITES

MAKES 1 BABY PORTION

	METRIC	IMPERIAL	AMERICAN
Medium carrot	1	1	1
Potato	100 g	4 oz	4 oz
Cooked chicken	50 g	2 oz	2 oz
Canned or frozen sweetcorn (corn)	15 ml	1 tbsp	1 tbsp
Egg yolk	1	1	1
Plain (all-purpose) flour	15 ml	1 tbsp	1 tbsp
Sunflower oil	30 ml	2 tbsp	2 tbsp

① Peel the carrot and potato and grate them coarsely. Squeeze out as much liquid as possible, then pat dry with kitchen paper (paper towels). Put in a bowl.

② Finely chop the chicken. Add to the grated vegetables with the sweetcorn and egg yolk. Mix well. Sprinkle over the flour and mix again.

③ Heat the oil in a large frying pan (skillet) over a medium heat. Drop spoonfuls of the mixture into the pan, lightly pressing down with the back of the spoon to flatten. Cook for about 3 minutes on each side until lightly browned and cooked through.

④ Drain on kitchen paper (paper towels) and allow to cool for a few minutes before serving.

FISHERMAN'S PIE

MAKES 2 ADULT PLUS 2 BABY PORTIONS

	METRIC	IMPERIAL	AMERICAN
Cod or haddock fillet	225 g	8 oz	8 oz
Milk	300 ml	½ pint	1¼ cups
Bay leaf	1	1	1
Small onion, sliced	1	1	1
Butter or margarine	40 g	1½ oz	3 tbsp
Plain (all-purpose) flour	30 ml	2 tbsp	2 tbsp
Egg, hard-boiled (hard-cooked) and finely chopped	1	1	1
Chopped fresh parsley	15 ml	1 tbsp	1 tbsp
Salt and freshly ground black pepper			
Potatoes, cut into chunks	225 g	8 oz	8 oz
Carrots, cut into chunks	100 g	4 oz	4 oz
Plain Greek yoghurt	30 ml	2 tbsp	2 tbsp

① Put the fish in a pan with the milk, bay leaf and onion. Slowly bring to boiling point, then simmer gently for 6 minutes or until the fish is opaque. Lift the fish from the pan using a slotted spoon and remove the skin and bones. Strain the milk and reserve.

② Melt 25 g/1 oz/2 tbsp of the butter or margarine in a pan. Stir in the flour and cook gently for 1 minute. Remove from the heat and gradually stir in the reserved milk. Bring to the boil and simmer for 2–3 minutes until thickened.

③ Stir the fish, egg and parsley into the sauce. Half-fill two 150 ml/¼ pint/⅔ cup ovenproof dishes with the fish mixture. Season the remainder with salt and pepper and spoon into an ovenproof pie dish.

④ Cook the potatoes and carrots in boiling water for 20 minutes until tender. Drain well and mash with the remaining butter or margarine and yoghurt. Spoon a little over the fish mixture in the individual dishes, then season the rest and use to top the fish in the pie dish.

⑤ Bake the baby portions in a preheated oven at 200°C/ 400°F/gas mark 6 for 15 minutes and the adults' pie for 20–25 minutes or until the tops are lightly browned.

⑥ Allow one of the baby portions to cool to the desired temperature before serving.

⑦ Cool the remaining portion, cover and freeze or store in the fridge for up to 24 hours.

Tip: If preferred, cook half the recipe quantity and divide it into eight baby-sized portions before freezing.

CHEESY COD AND BROCCOLI

MAKES 4 BABY PORTIONS

✿	METRIC	IMPERIAL	AMERICAN
Broccoli	100 g	4 oz	4 oz
Potato, diced	225 g	8 oz	8 oz
Frozen skinless cod	100 g	4 oz	4 oz
Milk	300 ml	½ pint	1¼ cups
Mild Cheddar cheese, grated	50 g	2 oz	½ cup

① Cut the broccoli into florets. Put it in a saucepan with the potato, cod and milk.

② Bring to the boil, simmer gently, uncovered, for 15 minutes or until the fish is cooked and the vegetables are tender. Remove from the heat, add the cheese and stir until melted.

③ Mash the mixture to the desired consistency. Spoon a portion into a bowl and allow to cool slightly, if necessary, before serving.

④ Cool the remaining purée, divide into portions and freeze, or cover and store in the fridge for up to 24 hours.

BUTTER BAKED SALMON WITH DILL SAUCE

MAKES 4 BABY PORTIONS

	METRIC	IMPERIAL	AMERICAN
Salmon fillet	100 g	4 oz	4 oz
Lemon juice	5 ml	1 tsp	1 tsp
Butter or margarine	25 g	1 oz	2 tbsp
Plain (all-purpose) flour	15 ml	1 tbsp	1 tbsp
Milk	120 ml	4 fl oz	½ cup
Finely chopped fresh dill (dill weed)	15 ml	1 tbsp	1 tbsp

① Put the salmon on a piece of foil, sprinkle with lemon juice and top with half of the butter or margarine. Bake in a preheated oven at 350°F/180°C/gas mark 4 for 15 minutes or until cooked through.

② Meanwhile, put the remaining butter or margarine, flour and milk in a small pan. Slowly bring to the boil, whisking all the time until smooth and thick. Simmer for 1 minute.

③ Strain the juices from the fish into the sauce. Flake the fish, then lightly mash with a fork, removing any skin and bones. Stir into the sauce with the dill.

④ Spoon a portion into a bowl and allow to cool slightly, if necessary, before serving.

⑤ Cool the remainder, divide into portions and freeze, or cover and store in the fridge for up to 24 hours.

CREAMY CARROT MOUSSE

This light, baked, savoury mousse makes a tasty vegetable accompaniment for adult meals too.

MAKES 4 BABY PORTIONS

✼	METRIC	IMPERIAL	AMERICAN
Carrots, roughly chopped	275 g	10 oz	10 oz
Small red (bell) pepper, halved, seeded and chopped	1	1	1
Vegetable stock (page 38) or water	45 ml	3 tbsp	3 tbsp
Eggs	2	2	2
Plain fromage frais	100 g	4 oz	½ cup

① Lightly grease four 150 ml/¼ pint/⅔ cup ramekins (custard cups) or small pudding basins and line the bases with greaseproof (waxed) paper.

② Put the chopped vegetables in a small saucepan with the stock or water. Cover and cook gently for 10 minutes or until very soft. Remove the lid for the last 2–3 minutes to allow the liquid to evaporate.

③ Sieve (strain) or purée the mixture in a food processor until fairly smooth.

④ Lightly whisk the eggs and fromage frais together. Stir in the vegetable purée. Divide the mixture between the prepared dishes, then cover each one with a piece of greased foil.

⑤ Put the dishes in a roasting tin (pan) and pour enough hot water into the tin to come about halfway up the dishes. Bake in a preheated oven at 180°C/350°F/gas mark 4 for 40 minutes or until lightly set.

⑥ Turn out one of the mousses into a bowl and allow to cool slightly, if necessary, before serving.

⑦ Cool the remaining mousses and freeze, or cover and store in the fridge for up to 24 hours.

PASTA PRIMAVERA

MAKES 4 BABY PORTIONS

	METRIC	IMPERIAL	AMERICAN
Ripe tomatoes	2	2	2
Medium carrot, diced	I	I	I
Small courgette (zucchini), diced	I	I	I
Green (French) beans, diced	25 g	I oz	I oz
Milk	250 ml	8 fl oz	I cup
Mini pasta shapes	40 g	I ½ oz	I ½ oz
Mild Cheddar cheese, finely grated	25 g	I oz	½ cup

① Plunge the tomatoes into boiling water. Leave for 1 minute, then remove and peel. Halve, seed and cut into tiny dice.

② Put the carrot, courgette and beans into a pan with the milk. Bring to the boil, part-cover with a lid and simmer for 10 minutes.

③ Add the tomatoes and pasta. Stir once, then simmer, uncovered, for a further 5 minutes until the pasta and vegetables are cooked. Remove from the heat, add the cheese and stir until melted.

④ Spoon a portion into a bowl and allow to cool slightly, if necessary, before serving.

⑤ Cool the remaining mixture, divide into portions and freeze, or cover and store in the fridge for up to 24 hours.

PASTA WITH MUSHROOM SAUCE

You can buy tiny pasta shapes, usually labelled 'mini' or 'soup' pasta, such as farfalline, which are ideal baby food as they don't need to be chewed.

MAKES I BABY PORTION

	METRIC	IMPERIAL	AMERICAN
Ripe tomato	I	I	I
Button mushrooms, finely chopped	3	3	3
Butter or margarine	15 g	½ oz	I tbsp
Mascarpone cheese	15 ml	I tbsp	I tbsp
Milk	30 ml	2 tbsp	2 tbsp
Mini pasta shapes	15 g	½ oz	½ oz

① Plunge the tomato into boiling water and leave for 1 minute. Remove, peel off the skin, halve, seed and finely chop. Wipe and chop the mushrooms.

② Melt the butter or margarine in a small saucepan. Add the mushrooms and gently cook for 3 minutes, then add the tomato and cook for a further 2–3 minutes or until very soft. Stir in the Mascarpone cheese and milk and heat until melted.

③ Meanwhile, cook the pasta in boiling water for 6 minutes until tender, or according to packet instructions. Drain well.

④ Stir the pasta into the mushroom sauce and spoon into a bowl. Allow to cool slightly, if necessary, before serving.

MAIN MEAL MINESTRONE

MAKES 2 ADULT PLUS I BABY PORTION

	METRIC	IMPERIAL	AMERICAN
Olive oil	15 ml	I tbsp	I tbsp
Rashers (slices) of streaky bacon, rinded and chopped	2	2	2
Large onion, chopped	I	I	I
Garlic clove, crushed	I	I	I
Medium carrots, finely diced	2	2	2
Celery sticks, diced	2	2	2
Medium potato, diced	I	I	I
A pinch of dried oregano			
Red wine (optional)	45 ml	3 tbsp	3 tbsp
Can of chopped tomatoes	200 g	7 oz	I small
Chicken stock	600 ml	I pint	2½ cups
Short-cut macaroni	40 g	1½ oz	1½ oz
Cooked chicken, skinned and finely chopped	100 g	4 oz	I cup
Salt and freshly ground black pepper			
Freshly grated Parmesan cheese, to serve			

① Heat the oil in a flameproof casserole dish (Dutch oven) or saucepan. Add the bacon and cook for a few minutes until crisp. Remove from the pan with a slotted spoon and set aside.

② Add the onion and garlic to the pan and gently fry (sauté) for 10 minutes until soft. Stir in the carrots, celery and potato and cook for a further 5 minutes, stirring all the time. Add the oregano, the wine, if using, and the tomatoes and stock.

③ Bring to the boil, turn down the heat, cover and simmer for 25 minutes. Add the macaroni and simmer, uncovered, for 8 minutes. Stir in the chicken and bacon and simmer for a further 2–3 minutes or until the pasta is tender.

④ Remove a portion of the minestrone for baby. Lightly mash with a fork, then allow it to cool slightly, if necessary, before serving.

⑤ Season the adult portions with salt and pepper and serve with freshly grated Parmesan cheese.

Tip: It's perfectly all right to add a little wine to a recipe like this, as all the alcohol evaporates during cooking.

SPAGHETTI JUNCTION

MAKES 4 BABY PORTIONS

✳	METRIC	IMPERIAL	AMERICAN
Milk	250 ml	8 fl oz	I cup
Fine quick-cook spaghetti	50 g	2 oz	2 oz
Frozen mixed vegetables	25 g	I oz	I oz
Wafer-thin slices of roast ham, finely chopped	50 g	2 oz	2 oz

① Bring the milk to the boil in a small saucepan. Break the spaghetti into short lengths, add to the milk and simmer, uncovered, for 4 minutes.

② Add the vegetables, part-cover with a lid and simmer for a further 5 minutes or until the spaghetti and vegetables are tender. Remove from the heat. Stir in the ham.

③ Lightly mash with a fork or purée to the desired consistency. Spoon a portion into a bowl and allow to cool slightly, if necessary, before serving.

④ Cool the remaining mixture, divide into portions and freeze, or cover and store in the fridge for up to 24 hours.

Tip: The spaghetti will absorb the milk as it cools and you may have to add a little extra milk when reheating from frozen.

SAVOURY SPINACH CUSTARD

MAKES I BABY PORTION

	METRIC	IMPERIAL	AMERICAN
Frozen spinach, thawed	50 g	2 oz	2 oz
Butter or margarine	15 g	½ oz	I tbsp
Egg	I	I	I
Milk	75 ml	5 tbsp	5 tbsp

① Thoroughly drain the spinach. Chop finely and put in a small pan with the butter or margarine. Cook gently for 3 minutes, until fairly dry. Remove from the heat and allow to cool for a few minutes.

② Whisk together the egg and milk. Stir into the spinach, then spoon the mixture into a greased 150 ml/¼ pint/⅔ cup ramekin (custard cup).

③ Bake in a preheated oven at 160°C/325°F/gas mark 3 for 30 minutes or until set. Allow to cool slightly before serving.

Tip: This recipe is also ideal for using up leftover vegetables, such as diced carrot or chopped cauliflower or broccoli.

CREAM CHEESE AND HAM PASTA

MAKES I BABY PORTION

	METRIC	IMPERIAL	AMERICAN
Wafer-thin slice of honey roast ham	I	I	I
Mini pasta shapes	15 g	½ oz	½ oz
Cream cheese	15 g	½ oz	I tbsp
Milk	15 ml	I tbsp	I tbsp

① Finely chop the ham. Cook the pasta in a small saucepan of boiling water for 5 minutes or until tender. Drain well.

② Heat the cream cheese and the milk in the pan, stirring until it melts to a sauce. Stir in the pasta and ham. Serve straight away.

FRENCH TOAST FINGERS

MAKES 1 BABY PORTION

	METRIC	IMPERIAL	AMERICAN
Slice of bread	1	1	1
Egg, beaten	½	½	½
Milk	15 ml	1 tbsp	1 tbsp
Butter or margarine	15 g	½ oz	1 tbsp
Sunflower oil	15 ml	1 tbsp	1 tbsp

1. Trim the crusts off the bread. Whisk the egg and milk together, then dip in the bread, turning after a few seconds to coat both sides.

2. Heat the butter or margarine and oil in a frying pan (skillet) until sizzling. Add the bread and cook for about 1½ minutes on each side or until golden brown.

3. Cool slightly, then cut into four strips. Serve as a meal or as finger food.

Tip: Put any remaining beaten egg in a small bowl, cover and store in the fridge for up to 24 hours.

CHOCOLATE DROP PUDDING

MAKES 1 BABY PORTION

	METRIC	IMPERIAL	AMERICAN
Ground rice	15 ml	1 tbsp	1 tbsp
Caster (superfine) sugar	5 ml	1 tsp	1 tsp
Milk	120 ml	4 fl oz	½ cup
Milk chocolate drops	25 g	1 oz	¼ cup

1. Put the rice and sugar in a small saucepan and gradually blend in the milk. Bring to the boil and simmer gently for 10–12 minutes, stirring occasionally, until the mixture has thickened and the rice is cooked. Remove from the heat and allow to cool for a few minutes.

2. Stir in the chocolate drops while the rice is still warm, then spoon into a bowl. Serve as the chocolate begins to melt.

VANILLA CREAMS

MAKES 2 BABY PORTIONS

	METRIC	IMPERIAL	AMERICAN
Caster (superfine) sugar	10 ml	2 tsp	2 tsp
Cornflour (cornstarch)	2.5 ml	½ tsp	½ tsp
Vanilla essence (extract)	1.5 ml	¼ tsp	¼ tsp
Egg	1	1	1
Milk	150 ml	¼ pint	⅔ cup

① Whisk the sugar, cornflour, vanilla essence and egg together in a jug. Pour the milk into a saucepan and heat to boiling point. Pour the milk over the egg mixture, whisking all the time.

② Divide the mixture between two lightly greased ramekins (custard cups) and place in a roasting tin (pan). Pour enough warm water into the tin to come about halfway up the ramekins.

③ Bake in a preheated oven at 180°C/350°F/gas mark 4 for 20 minutes or until the custard is just set. Remove from the water and leave to cool. Serve one portion at room temperature.

④ Cover and chill the remaining custard cream. Serve cold within 24 hours. Do not reheat.

FRESH FRUITY JELLY

MAKES 2–3 BABY PORTIONS

	METRIC	IMPERIAL	AMERICAN
Fresh fruit juice, such as orange	300 ml	½ pint	1¼ cups
Powdered gelatine	10 ml	2 tsp	2 tsp

① Spoon 60 ml/4 tbsp of the fruit juice into a small bowl. Sprinkle the gelatine over and leave to soak for 5 minutes. Place the bowl over a pan of near-boiling water until the gelatine has dissolved, stirring occasionally. Cool for a few minutes, then stir the dissolved gelatine into the rest of the juice.

② Divide between two or three individual dishes. Chill in the fridge for at least 3 hours, or overnight if preferred, until set.

③ Remove one portion from the fridge about 20 minutes before serving to take the chill off.

④ Cover the remaining portion(s) and store in the fridge for up to 48 hours.

Tip: Use any of your baby's favourite fruit juices, such as apple, peach or tropical fruit. If liked, make a Fruit and Fromage Frais Jelly by substituting 150 ml/¼ pint/⅔ cup of the fruit juice with plain or fruit-flavoured fromage frais. Serve within 24 hours of making.

CHOCOLATE MILK JELLY

MAKES 2 BABY PORTIONS

	METRIC	IMPERIAL	AMERICAN
Milk	200 ml	7 fl oz	scant 1 cup
Powdered gelatine	5 ml	1 tsp	1 tsp
Cocoa (unsweetened chocolate) powder	5 ml	1 tsp	1 tsp
Caster (superfine) sugar	5 ml	1 tsp	1 tsp

① Spoon 30 ml/2 tbsp milk into a small bowl and sprinkle over the gelatine. Leave to soak for 5 minutes. Place over a pan of near-boiling water until dissolved, stirring occasionally.

② Meanwhile, blend the cocoa powder and sugar with a little of the remaining milk in a small saucepan. Whisk in all of the remaining milk and bring to the boil. Remove from the heat.

③ Add the soaked gelatine to the chocolate milk and stir until dissolved. Pour into two small dishes or jelly moulds. Allow to cool, then put in the fridge to set.

④ Remove one portion from the fridge about 20 minutes before serving, to take the chill off.

⑤ Cover the remaining portion and serve within 24 hours.

Tip: The jelly can be served in the dishes or turned out if preferred. Dip the dishes in very hot water for a few seconds to loosen, place a plate or bowl on top of the dish and invert.

STEAMED BANANA CUSTARD

MAKES 1 BABY PORTION

	METRIC	IMPERIAL	AMERICAN
Ripe banana	½	½	½
Egg	1	1	1
Milk	45 ml	3 tbsp	3 tbsp
Caster (superfine) sugar	2.5 ml	½ tsp	½ tsp
A few drops of vanilla essence (extract)			

① Peel and thinly slice the banana and place in a greased 150 ml/¼ pint/⅔ cup ramekin (custard cup).

② Whisk the egg, milk, sugar and vanilla essence together. Pour over the banana slices. Cover with a piece of foil and place in a steamer.

③ Cover and steam over gently boiling water for about 15 minutes, until set. Allow to cool slightly before serving.

APRICOT FOOL

MAKES 4 BABY PORTIONS

❋ (SEE TIP)	METRIC	IMPERIAL	AMERICAN
Dried apricots	100 g	4 oz	⅔ cup
Apple or peach juice	150 ml	¼ pint	⅔ cup
Plain Greek yoghurt, to serve			

① Rinse the apricots under cold running water to remove any preservative. Chop finely and put in a small saucepan with the apple or peach juice. Leave to soak for at least 2 hours.

② Cook over a gentle heat for 4–5 minutes or until the apricots are very soft. Purée until smooth. Leave to cool.

③ Spoon a quarter of the apricot purée into a bowl and stir in 15 ml/1 tbsp of Greek yoghurt.

④ Divide the remaining purée into portions and freeze, or cover and store in the fridge for up to 24 hours.

Tip: Freeze the apricot purée without the yoghurt.

FROM BABY TO TODDLER

Your child is now nearing the stage when she will eat more or less the same sort of food as the rest of the family and there's no longer any need to purée her meals. Encourage her to become familiar with a wide variety of foods. You may wish to give 'follow-on' milk for a few more months, or to switch to full-fat cows' milk; skimmed and semi-skimmed milk and low-fat foods should be avoided until the age of two, as they don't have the concentration of calories needed by young children and have less of the vitamins A and D. Try to cook healthily though, by trimming fat from meat and cooking with vegetable rather than saturated animal fats. You should also avoid too many meals of fried (sautéed) food, processed meat like salami, sausages and pies, and frequent high-fat snacks such as crisps (chips) and chocolate. You'll find a selection of desserts and bakes in this chapter; serve them as occasional treats rather than daily – fresh and dried fruit, yoghurt and fromage frais are all easy and healthy alternatives.

FUSSY EATERS

Nearly all children are fickle eaters at times and quickly learn to assert themselves and to let you know what they do and don't like. They may have a fad which goes on for days or even weeks and the lovingly prepared food they enjoyed yesterday may be rejected today. This can be very trying for you, but try to respect your baby's individuality, within reason, and to find alternatives to the foods that are refused. If milk is turned down, offer yoghurt or flavoured milk jelly; if she's eating plenty of fruit, it really doesn't matter if she leaves all her vegetables. Think of food intake on a weekly rather than a daily basis; hopefully if your child rejects a meal one day, she'll make up for it the next. A balanced diet over several weeks is perfectly beneficial. If your child refuses a meal (assuming you haven't given her something you know she doesn't like), don't rush away and prepare an alternative or offer sweets and biscuits later or she'll soon discover that this is a good ploy to get what she wants. If you're worried that your child is really hungry, bring the next meal time forward. If that's not convenient, offer some toast or bread and butter or margarine. If your toddler is going through a 'picky' phase, don't spend hours in the kitchen preparing meals; choose something quick and easy, or you'll end up even more frustrated when she refuses to eat. Try to accept that toddlers' appetites are unpredictable and there will inevitably be days when they eat practically nothing.

Children often dislike the texture of meat. Try finely minced (ground) meats instead, but if your child refuses these as well, don't worry, as there are plenty of other good sources of protein, such as dairy produce and eggs. Protein is also found in reasonable quantities in pulses (beans and lentils), peanut butter and bread.

Encourage an interest in food by making it look as attractive as possible. Try arranging it in patterns or make it look like a face, if you have the time and patience. Otherwise, adding eyes, nose and a smiling mouth in ketchup (catsup) sometimes works wonders!

EASY CHEESE AND TOMATO PIZZA PUFFS

MAKES 2 ADULT PLUS 1 BABY PORTION

	METRIC	IMPERIAL	AMERICAN
Puff pastry (paste)	350 g	12 oz	12 oz
Sun-dried tomato purée (paste)	45 ml	3 tbsp	3 tbsp
Mascarpone cheese	30 ml	2 tbsp	2 tbsp
A pinch of dried mixed herbs			
Cheddar cheese, finely grated	75 g	3 oz	¾ cup
Cherry tomatoes, halved	15	15	15

① Roll out the pastry on a lightly floured work surface and cut out five 12 cm/5 in rounds using a small plate or saucer as a guide. Transfer to a lightly greased baking (cookie) sheet and prick all over with a fork. Chill in the fridge for 20 minutes.

② Mix together the tomato purée, Mascarpone and herbs. Spread evenly over the pastry bases. Sprinkle half the grated cheese over the top, then arrange the cherry tomatoes over it, cut-sides up. Sprinkle with the remaining cheese.

③ Bake on the middle shelf in a preheated oven at 220°C/425°F/gas mark 7 for 14–15 minutes or until the pastry is golden and crisp and the cheese lightly browned and bubbling.

④ Allow to cool on the baking sheet for a few minutes – the cheese and tomatoes will be very hot. Serve two pizza puffs for each adult and one for baby.

CREAMY CHICKEN KORMA

This very mild curry is a great introduction to spicy foods and you can jazz up the adults' servings with some hot Indian pickles.

MAKES 2 ADULT PLUS 1 BABY PORTION

	METRIC	IMPERIAL	AMERICAN
Ghee or sunflower oil	15 ml	1 tbsp	1 tbsp
Large onion, finely chopped	1	1	1
Garlic clove, crushed	1	1	1
Ground coriander (cilantro)	5 ml	1 tsp	1 tsp
Ground ginger	1.5 ml	¼ tsp	¼ tsp
Ground cumin	1.5 ml	¼ tsp	¼ tsp
Boneless chicken breasts, skinned	2	2	2
Lemon juice	5 ml	1 tsp	1 tsp
Thick plain yoghurt	400 ml	14 fl oz	1¾ cups
Chicken or vegetable stock (page 38)	75 ml	5 tbsp	5 tbsp
Salt and freshly ground black pepper			
Rice or naan bread, to serve			

① Heat the ghee or oil in a saucepan and gently fry (sauté) the onion for 5 minutes. Add the garlic and cook for a further 5 minutes or until the onion is soft and just beginning to colour. Stir in the spices and cook, stirring all the time, for 1 minute.

② Meanwhile, cut each chicken breast into four pieces. Add to the pan with the lemon juice. Turn the heat down as low as possible, then stir in three-quarters of the yoghurt, a spoonful at a time.

③ Stir in the stock. Part-cover the pan with a lid and simmer gently for about 30 minutes until the chicken is very tender and cooked through.

④ Remove one or two pieces of chicken for baby and chop very finely. Put in a bowl and mix with a spoonful of the sauce and a little extra yoghurt. Stir in a spoonful of rice or serve with strips of warmed naan bread.

⑤ Season the remaining korma with salt and pepper and serve to the adults topped with a drizzle of yoghurt and some hot pickles and rice or naan bread.

Tip: Choose Bio or Greek-style yoghurt for this recipe as it has a creamier, less tangy flavour than ordinary yoghurt.

CRUNCHY CHICKEN NUGGETS

MAKES 6 BABY PORTIONS

❄	METRIC	IMPERIAL	AMERICAN
Skinless chicken breast	225 g	8 oz	8 oz
Fresh white breadcrumbs	50 g	2 oz	1 cup
Cooked long-grain rice	100 g	4 oz	1 cup
Egg, beaten	1	1	1
Chopped fresh parsley (optional)	15 ml	1 tbsp	1 tbsp
Salt and freshly ground black pepper			
Plain (all-purpose) flour	25 g	1 oz	¼ cup
Sunflower oil	30 ml	2 tbsp	2 tbsp

① Roughly chop the chicken and process in a food processor until just smooth. Alternatively, chop very finely.

② Transfer the chicken to a bowl. Add the breadcrumbs, rice, egg and parsley, if using. Lightly season with salt and pepper and mix well.

③ Using floured hands, shape into 18 equal-sized balls and place on a baking (cookie) tray.

④ Heat the oil in a frying pan (skillet) and cook three of the chicken nuggets for about 6 minutes, turning until browned all over and cooked through. Allow to cool slightly before serving.

⑤ Open-freeze the remaining nuggets, then pack in portions in freezerproof containers or bags.

CRUMBLE-TOPPED LAMB CASSEROLE

MAKES 2 ADULT PLUS 1 BABY PORTION

	METRIC	IMPERIAL	AMERICAN
Lean lamb, such as boned leg or shoulder	350 g	12 oz	12 oz
Sunflower oil	30 ml	2 tbsp	2 tbsp
Onion, finely chopped	I	I	I
Plain (all-purpose) flour	15 ml	1 tbsp	1 tbsp
Lamb or vegetable stock (page 38)	150 ml	¼ pint	⅔ cup
Carrots, diced	175 g	6 oz	6 oz
Turnips, diced	175 g	6 oz	6 oz
Can of chopped tomatoes	200 g	7 oz	1 small
Dried thyme	2.5 ml	½ tsp	½ tsp
Bay leaf	I	I	I
Salt and freshly ground black pepper			
For the topping:			
Plain (all-purpose) flour	100 g	4 oz	1 cup
Butter or margarine	50 g	2 oz	¼ cup
Cheddar cheese, finely grated	50 g	2 oz	½ cup

① Trim any fat from the lamb and cut into tiny cubes. Heat the oil in a 1.75 litre/3 pint/7½ cup flameproof casserole (Dutch oven) and fry (sauté) the lamb until lightly browned. Remove from the casserole with a slotted spoon.

② Add the onion to the casserole and fry for 5 minutes, until beginning to soften and brown. Sprinkle over the flour and stir in. Gradually add the stock, then stir in the carrots, turnips, chopped tomatoes, herbs and a little seasoning.

③ Bring to the boil, stirring occasionally. Cover and cook in a preheated oven at 160°C/325°F/gas mark 3 for 1 hour. Turn up the oven to 180°C/350°F/gas mark 5.

④ Sift the flour for the topping into a bowl. Cut the butter or margarine into small cubes and rub in until the mixture resembles breadcrumbs. Stir in the grated cheese. Sprinkle the topping over the casserole, return to the oven and cook, uncovered, for a further 30–35 minutes or until lightly browned. Cool the baby portion before serving.

CHICKEN SATAY STICKS

These tasty chicken skewers make ideal finger food, but remember to remove the meat from the skewers and take them away before serving. Do read the section on allergies on page 16 before giving peanut butter to your baby.

MAKES 2 ADULT PLUS I BABY PORTION

	METRIC	IMPERIAL	AMERICAN
Skinless chicken breast	350 g	12 oz	12 oz
Sesame oil	10 ml	2 tsp	2 tsp
Sunflower oil	15 ml	1 tbsp	1 tbsp
Lemon juice	10 ml	2 tsp	2 tsp
Soy sauce	10 ml	2 tsp	2 tsp
Clear honey	15 ml	1 tbsp	1 tbsp
For the peanut dip:			
Creamed coconut	25 g	1 oz	1 oz
Water	75 ml	5 tbsp	5 tbsp
Small pinch of mild chilli powder			
Smooth peanut butter	50 g	2 oz	4 tbsp
Soft dark brown sugar	10 ml	2 tsp	2 tsp
Lemon juice	5 ml	1 tsp	1 tsp

① Cut the chicken into cubes. Mix together the oils, lemon juice, soy sauce and honey. Add the chicken, toss to coat, then cover and marinate in the fridge for 2 hours.

② Meanwhile, make the peanut dip. Roughly chop the creamed coconut and put in a small pan with the water. Heat gently until melted. Stir in the chilli powder, peanut butter, sugar and lemon juice. Stir until combined, then spoon into a serving bowl.

③ Thread the chicken on to skewers. Cook under a hot grill (broiler) for 8–10 minutes, turning occasionally and brushing with the marinade, until cooked through.

④ Serve the chicken satay warm or cold with the peanut dip.

LAMB AND LENTIL LASAGNE

MAKES 2 ADULT PLUS 1 BABY PORTION

	METRIC	IMPERIAL	AMERICAN
Olive oil	15 ml	1 tbsp	1 tbsp
Onion, finely chopped	1	1	1
Lean minced (ground) lamb	225 g	8 oz	8 oz
Dried oregano	2.5 ml	½ tsp	½ tsp
Plain (all-purpose) flour	40 g	1½ oz	⅓ cup
Lamb or vegetable stock (page 38)	150 ml	¼ pint	⅔ cup
Tomato purée (paste)	15 ml	1 tbsp	1 tbsp
Red lentils	30 ml	2 tbsp	2 tbsp
Salt and freshly ground black pepper			
Butter or margarine	25 g	1 oz	2 tbsp
Milk	300 ml	½ pint	1¼ cups
Cheddar cheese, finely grated	75 g	3 oz	¾ cup
No-need-to-pre-cook lasagne sheets	6	6	6

① Heat the oil in a saucepan and gently cook the onion for 10 minutes until soft and just beginning to brown. Remove from the pan and set aside.

② Add the lamb to the pan and cook until browned. Pour off any excess fat. Return the onion to the pan with the oregano. Sprinkle over 15 ml/1 tbsp of the flour and stir in. Gradually add the stock, tomato purée, lentils and a little salt and pepper. Cover and simmer for 20 minutes.

③ Meanwhile, put the remaining flour, the butter or margarine and milk in a saucepan and slowly bring to the boil, stirring all the time until thickened and smooth. Remove from the heat and stir in 50 g/2 oz/½ cup of the cheese.

④ Layer the lamb mixture alternately with the lasagne sheets in a lightly greased, deep, ovenproof serving dish. Spoon over the cheese sauce, then sprinkle with the remaining cheese.

⑤ Bake in a preheated oven at 190°C/375°F/gas mark 5 for 35 minutes or until the lasagne is cooked and the topping brown and bubbling.

6. Spoon the baby portion into a bowl and chop the lasagne into small pieces. Allow to cool to the desired temperature before serving.

CRUNCHY FISH FINGERS

Do read the section on allergies on page 16 before giving sesame seeds to your child.

MAKES 3 BABY PORTIONS

❄	METRIC	IMPERIAL	AMERICAN
Plaice fillets	350 g	12 oz	12 oz
Plain (all-purpose) flour	30 ml	2 tbsp	2 tbsp
Egg	1	1	1
Fresh white breadcrumbs	75 g	3 oz	¾ cup
Sesame seeds	15 ml	1 tbsp	1 tbsp
Mashed potatoes or chips (fries) and a green vegetable, to serve			

1. Skin the plaice, rinse under cold water and pat dry on kitchen paper (paper towels). Cut into thin strips and toss in the flour, to coat.

2. Lightly beat the egg. Mix together the breadcrumbs and sesame seeds and place on a plate. Dip the floured fish strips, one at a time, in the egg, then in the breadcrumbs. Place one-third of the fish fingers on a lightly greased baking (cookie) sheet.

3. Bake in a preheated oven at 200°C/400°F/gas mark 6 for about 12 minutes or until crisp and golden brown. Serve straight away with mashed potatoes or chips and a green vegetable.

4. Put the remaining fish fingers on a baking sheet and open-freeze until solid. Remove from the tray, place in a freezerproof container or bag and freeze until required.

Tip: Make sure that you buy fresh plaice fillets that have not been previously frozen.

CHICKEN GOUJONS WITH CHUNKY OVEN FRIES

MAKES 3 BABY PORTIONS OF GOUJONS

✳ (GOUJONS)	METRIC	IMPERIAL	AMERICAN
For the goujons:			
Skinless chicken breast	175 g	6 oz	6 oz
Plain (all-purpose) flour	30 ml	2 tbsp	2 tbsp
A pinch of dried thyme (optional)			
Egg, beaten	1	1	1
Fresh white breadcrumbs	50 g	2 oz	1 cup
For the chunky oven fries:			
Potato, cut into fingers	100 g	4 oz	4 oz
Sunflower oil	15 ml	1 tbsp	1 tbsp
Baked beans in tomato sauce or peas, to serve			

① Cut the chicken breast into strips about 4 cm/1½ in long. Mix together the flour and thyme, if using. Dip the chicken strips in the flour, then in beaten egg and finally in breadcrumbs. Place one-third of the goujons on a lightly greased baking (cookie) tray.

② Add the potato fingers to a pan of boiling water and simmer for 3 minutes. Drain well.

③ Return the potato fingers to the pan and drizzle over the oil. Toss until lightly coated. Place in a single layer on the baking tray, next to the goujons.

④ Bake on the top shelf of a preheated oven at 200°C/400°F/ gas mark 6 for 15 minutes, turning the chicken and chips (fries) once, or until the chicken is cooked through and the chips are crisp and golden.

⑤ Transfer to a plate and allow to cool slightly before serving with baked beans or peas.

⑥ Divide the uncooked goujons into two portions. Open-freeze until solid, then put in freezerproof containers or bags and freeze until required. Alternatively, cover and store in the fridge for up to 24 hours.

MINI MEATBALLS IN RICH TOMATO SAUCE

MAKES 2 ADULT PLUS 2 BABY PORTIONS

❄	METRIC	IMPERIAL	AMERICAN
Lean minced (ground) beef	350 g	12 oz	12 oz
Fresh white breadcrumbs	50 g	2 oz	1 cup
Egg yolk	1	1	1
Chopped fresh parsley	15 ml	1 tbsp	1 tbsp
Salt and freshly ground black pepper			
Olive oil	15 ml	1 tbsp	1 tbsp
Medium onion, finely chopped	1	1	1
Garlic clove, crushed	1	1	1
Can of chopped tomatoes	400 g	14 oz	1 large
Dried mixed herbs	2.5 ml	½ tsp	½ tsp
Pasta or rice, to serve			

1. Mix together the beef, breadcrumbs, egg yolk and parsley. Season with a little salt and pepper. With dampened hands, shape the mixture into 12 small balls.

2. Heat the oil in a frying pan (skillet), add the meatballs and cook over a medium heat for 5 minutes, turning frequently until browned all over. Remove from the pan with a slotted spoon and set aside.

3. Add the onion and garlic to the pan and gently cook for 10 minutes until soft. Stir in the tomatoes and dried herbs and season with a little salt and pepper. Bring to the boil, cover and simmer for 10 minutes.

4. Place the meatballs in the sauce. Cover and simmer for a further 15 minutes or until cooked through.

5. Spoon a little of the sauce into a bowl and top with two meatballs. Allow to cool slightly before serving. Remove a second baby portion, cool and freeze or cover and store in the fridge for up to 24 hours.

6. Divide the remaining sauce and meatballs between the adults and serve with pasta or rice.

Tip: If preferred, the recipe can be divided into six baby portions.

SIMPLE SWEET AND SOUR CHICKEN

MAKES 2 ADULT PLUS 1 BABY PORTION

❋	METRIC	IMPERIAL	AMERICAN
Sunflower oil	15 ml	1 tbsp	1 tbsp
Skinless chicken breasts, cubed	2	2	2
Cornflour (cornstarch)	10 ml	2 tsp	2 tsp
Sherry or white wine vinegar	10 ml	2 tsp	2 tsp
Light soy sauce	10 ml	2 tsp	2 tsp
Can of crushed pineapple	250 g	9 oz	1 small
Tomato ketchup (catsup)	15 ml	1 tbsp	1 tbsp
Clear honey	5 ml	1 tsp	1 tsp
Medium carrot, diced	1	1	1
Broccoli, cut into tiny florets	175 g	6 oz	6 oz
Salt and freshly ground black pepper			
Plain boiled rice or noodles, to serve			

① Heat the oil in a frying pan (skillet) and gently fry (sauté) the chicken for 5 minutes or until lightly browned. Remove from the pan and set aside.

② Blend the cornflour with the sherry or vinegar and soy sauce. Add to the pan with the pineapple, ketchup and honey. Bring to the boil, stirring until thickened. Add the carrot and broccoli and simmer for 3 minutes.

③ Return the chicken and any juices to the pan and simmer for a further 4–5 minutes or until the vegetables are tender and the chicken cooked through.

④ Spoon a baby portion into a bowl and chop up the chicken into tiny pieces. Stir in a spoonful of rice or chopped noodles and leave to cool to the desired temperature before serving.

⑤ Season the remaining sweet and sour chicken with salt and pepper. Spoon on to a bed of rice or noodles and serve straight away.

Tip: If preferred, halve the recipe quantity, divide into five baby portions and freeze, or cover and store in the fridge for up to 24 hours.

SPECIAL FRIED RICE

MAKES 2 ADULT PLUS 1 BABY PORTION

	METRIC	IMPERIAL	AMERICAN
Long-grain rice	225 g	8 oz	1 cup
Sesame oil	5 ml	1 tsp	1 tsp
Sunflower oil	30 ml	2 tbsp	2 tbsp
Spring onions (scallions), thinly sliced	6	6	6
Medium carrot, coarsely grated	1	1	1
Beansprouts	100 g	4 oz	4 oz
Frozen peas	50 g	2 oz	2 oz
Small cooked peeled prawns (shrimp)	100 g	4 oz	4 oz
Light soy sauce	15 ml	1 tbsp	1 tbsp
Chilli sauce, to serve (optional)			

① Cook the rice in lightly salted boiling water for 8 minutes or until just tender. Drain well, rinse with boiling water, then drain again. Set aside.

② Heat the oils in a wok or large frying pan (skillet). Add the spring onions and carrot and stir-fry for 2 minutes. Add the beansprouts and peas and stir-fry for 1 further minute.

③ Add the rice, prawns and soy sauce. Stir-fry for a further 3 minutes or until the rice and prawns are heated through.

④ Spoon a baby-sized portion into a bowl and allow to cool slightly before serving.

⑤ Divide the remainder between the adults and serve sprinkled with a little chilli sauce, if liked.

SAUSAGE BALLS

MAKES 4 BABY PORTIONS

❄	METRIC	IMPERIAL	AMERICAN
Spring onion (scallion), finely chopped	I	I	I
Good-quality sausagemeat	225 g	8 oz	8 oz
Worcestershire sauce	5 ml	I tsp	I tsp
Tomato purée (paste)	5 ml	I tsp	I tsp
Plain (all-purpose) flour	10 ml	2 tsp	2 tsp
Sesame seeds	30 ml	2 tbsp	2 tbsp
Sunflower oil	30 ml	2 tbsp	2 tbsp
Mashed potatoes and baked beans in tomato sauce or peas, to serve			

① Put the spring onion in a bowl with the sausagemeat, Worcestershire sauce and tomato purée and mix together well. Shape the mixture into 20 bite-sized balls.

② Mix the flour and sesame seeds in a small bowl. Roll the sausage balls in the seed mixture a few at a time until coated.

③ Heat the oil in a frying pan (skillet) and fry (sauté) five of the sausage balls for 5–6 minutes, turning frequently until browned all over. Serve warm with mashed potatoes and baked beans or peas, or cold as finger food.

④ Open-freeze the remaining sausage balls until solid, then divide into portions, pack in freezerproof bags or containers and freeze until required.

Tip: When using the frozen portions, separate the sausage balls while still frozen and allow to defrost on a plate before cooking.

COD CREOLE

Creole is a delicious Caribbean style of cooking in which the food is prepared with peppers, tomatoes and rice. The usual dash of hot and spicy Tabasco sauce has been left out of this recipe!

MAKES 3 BABY PORTIONS

✿	METRIC	IMPERIAL	AMERICAN
Vegetable stock (page 38)	300 ml	½ pint	1¼ cups
Tomato purée (paste)	5 ml	1 tsp	1 tsp
Red (bell) pepper, seeded and finely chopped	½	½	½
Long-grain rice	50 g	2 oz	¼ cup
Skinless cod	100 g	4 oz	4 oz

① Pour the stock into a small saucepan, add the tomato purée and bring to the boil. Add the pepper, rice and fish, then turn down the heat.

② Part-cover the pan with a lid, then simmer gently for 15 minutes or until the rice and fish are cooked.

③ Lift out the fish with a slotted spoon and flake, discarding any bones. Stir the flaked fish back into the rice mixture and spoon one-third into a bowl. Cool slightly, if necessary, before serving.

④ Divide the rest of the mixture into portions, cover and freeze, or store in the fridge for up to 24 hours.

TODDLER TUNA TAGLIATELLE

MAKES 2 ADULT PLUS 1 BABY PORTION

	METRIC	IMPERIAL	AMERICAN
Olive oil	30 ml	2 tbsp	2 tbsp
Small onion, finely chopped	1	1	1
Celery stick, finely chopped	1	1	1
Garlic clove, crushed	1	1	1
Can of chopped tomatoes	200 g	7 oz	1 small
Vegetable stock (page 38)	100 ml	3½ fl oz	scant ½ cup
Bay leaf	1	1	1
Can of tuna in oil	200 g	7 oz	1 small
Tagliatelle	200 g	7 oz	7 oz
Butter or margarine	15 g	½ oz	1 tbsp
Snipped fresh chives	15 ml	1 tbsp	1 tbsp
Salt and freshly ground black pepper			
Finely grated Parmesan cheese, to serve (optional)			

1. Heat the oil in a small saucepan and gently cook the onion and celery for 5 minutes. Add the garlic and cook for a further 5 minutes until soft.

2. Stir in the chopped tomatoes, stock and bay leaf. Bring to the boil, then turn down the heat. Part-cover with a lid and simmer for 20 minutes. Remove the bay leaf. Drain the tuna and flake. Stir into the sauce and heat for 1–2 minutes.

3. Meanwhile, cook the tagliatelle in boiling salted water for 10 minutes, or according to the packet instructions. Drain thoroughly and toss in the butter or margarine and chives.

5. Spoon a little tagliatelle into a bowl and cut into small pieces. Top with a little of the sauce and allow to cool slightly before serving.

5. Season the remaining sauce with salt and freshly ground black pepper and serve to the adults with the tagliatelle. Sprinkle with Parmesan cheese, if liked.

PLAICE WITH CARROT AND ORANGE SAUCE

MAKES 2 ADULT PLUS 1 BABY PORTION

	METRIC	IMPERIAL	AMERICAN
Small plaice fillets	5	5	5
Vegetable stock (page 38)	300 ml	½ pint	1¼ pints
Salt and freshly ground black pepper			
Carrots, roughly chopped	175 g	6 oz	6 oz
Juice of ½ orange			
Bay leaf	1	1	1
Sprigs of coriander (cilantro)	2	2	2
Cornflour (cornstarch)	15 ml	1 tbsp	1 tbsp
Plain Greek yoghurt	60 ml	4 tbsp	4 tbsp
Chopped fresh coriander (cilantro)	15 ml	1 tbsp	1 tbsp

① Skin the plaice fillets and rinse under cold water. Trim and roll up neatly, starting at the wider end, and with the skinned side to the outside. Put in a lightly greased ovenproof dish. Spoon over 60 ml/4 tbsp of the stock, season lightly and cover with foil.

② Put the carrots in a saucepan with the orange juice, the remaining stock, the bay leaf and sprigs of coriander. Bring to the boil, turn down the heat, cover and simmer for 20 minutes until tender.

③ Meanwhile, put the fish in a preheated oven at 190°C/375°F/gas mark 5 and bake for 15–20 minutes or until cooked.

④ Remove the bay leaf and coriander sprigs from the carrots, then purée until smooth. Rinse out the pan. Blend the cornflour and yoghurt together in the pan, then stir in the carrot purée. Reheat gently until thickened, stirring continuously.

⑤ Serve two plaice fillets for each adult and one for baby. Spoon over the carrot sauce and sprinkle with the chopped coriander.

ESKIMO'S SPECIAL SUPPER

MAKES 2 ADULT PLUS 1 BABY PORTION

	METRIC	IMPERIAL	AMERICAN
New potatoes, scrubbed	350 g	12 oz	12 oz
Butter or margarine	25 g	1 oz	2 tbsp
Plain (all-purpose) flour	25 g	1 oz	¼ cup
Milk	250 ml	8 fl oz	1 cup
Smoked cod or haddock, skinned and boned	225 g	8 oz	8 oz
Freshly ground black pepper			
Red Leicester cheese, finely grated	50 g	2 oz	½ cup

① Cook the potatoes in boiling salted water for 15 minutes. Drain and leave until cool enough to handle, then slice.

② Put the butter or margarine, flour and milk in a saucepan and slowly bring to the boil, stirring all the time until smooth and thickened.

③ Cut the fish into small cubes and stir into the sauce. Simmer for 4–5 minutes until the fish is cooked. Remove from the heat and stir in three-quarters of the cheese.

④ Spoon a little of the fish mixture into a greased 150 ml/ ¼ pint/⅔ cup ramekin (custard cup). Season the remainder with pepper and spoon into a 750 ml/1¼ pint/3 cup shallow flameproof dish.

⑤ Lay the potato slices over the fish in both dishes and sprinkle with the remaining cheese. Place under a medium grill (broiler) for 4–5 minutes until the potatoes and cheese are golden brown and bubbling. Cool the baby portion to the desired temperature before serving.

FLUFFY CHEESE ON TOAST

MAKES I LARGE BABY PORTION

	METRIC	IMPERIAL	AMERICAN
Butter or margarine	15 g	½ oz	I tbsp
Plain (all-purpose) flour	10 ml	2 tsp	2 tsp
Milk	75 ml	5 tbsp	5 tbsp
Cheddar cheese, finely grated	25 g	I oz	¼ cup
Egg, separated	I	I	I
Slices of toast	2	2	2

1. Melt the butter or margarine in a small saucepan over a gentle heat. Stir in the flour and cook for a few seconds. Add the milk, a little at a time. Simmer for 1 minute, until thickened, then remove from the heat.

2. Stir in the cheese until melted, then the egg yolk. Whisk the egg white until stiff and fold into the mixture.

3. Spoon the mixture on top of the toast and cook under a low grill (broiler) for 4–5 minutes until cooked through, golden brown and puffy. Cool for a few minutes before serving.

EGG IN A BASKET

MAKES 1 BABY PORTION

	METRIC	IMPERIAL	AMERICAN
Slice of white or wholemeal bread	1	1	1
Butter or margarine	15 g	½ oz	1 tbsp
Egg	1	1	1
Milk	15 ml	1 tbsp	1 tbsp

①   Remove the crusts from the bread and thinly spread both sides with most of the butter or margarine. Press the bread into a patty tin (pan) to form a basket. Bake in a preheated oven at 200°C/400°F/gas mark 6 for 8 minutes or until lightly browned.

②   Meanwhile, melt the remaining butter or margarine in a small pan. Whisk together the egg and milk and pour into the pan. Cook over a gentle heat, stirring all the time until lightly set.

③   Place the bread basket on a plate and spoon in the scrambled egg. Serve straight away.

Tip: Flavour the scrambled egg by stirring in a skinned, seeded and diced tomato or a chopped thin slice of ham.

BACON AND TOMATO SCRAMBLE

MAKES 1 BABY PORTION

	METRIC	IMPERIAL	AMERICAN
Rasher (slice) of streaky bacon, rinded	1	1	1
Ripe tomato	1	1	1
Egg	1	1	1
Milk	15 ml	1 tbsp	1 tbsp
Butter or margarine	15 g	½ oz	1 tbsp
Fingers of hot buttered toast, to serve			

① Chop the bacon into small pieces. Dry-fry in a small non-stick frying pan (skillet) for 3–4 minutes until crisp. Remove and set aside.

② Meanwhile, plunge the tomato into boiling water for 1 minute. Remove, then peel, halve and remove the seeds. Finely chop the flesh.

③ Beat the egg with the milk. Melt the butter or margarine in the frying pan over a low heat, then add the egg mixture and chopped tomato. Cook slowly, stirring all the time, until thickened and set. Spoon on to a plate.

④ Sprinkle over the bacon pieces and allow to cool for a minute or two. Serve with fingers of buttered toast.

SQUEAKIES

These mini 'bubble and squeak' fritters may be served as finger food or as part of a meal.

MAKES 1 BABY PORTION

	METRIC	IMPERIAL	AMERICAN
Potato, coarsely grated	100 g	4 oz	4 oz
Cooked cabbage, finely chopped	50 g	2 oz	2 oz
Frozen peas, defrosted	15 ml	1 tbsp	1 tbsp
Plain (all-purpose) flour	30 ml	2 tbsp	2 tbsp
Egg	1	1	1
Sunflower oil	30 ml	2 tbsp	2 tbsp

① Squeeze any excess liquid out of the potato, then pat dry on kitchen paper (paper towels).

② Add the cabbage and peas to the grated potato. Sprinkle over the flour and mix together. Add the egg and mix again.

③ Heat the oil in a frying pan (skillet) and drop in tablespoonfuls of the mixture. Flatten with the back of a fork and cook for 4–5 minutes on each side until crisp and golden.

④ Drain on kitchen paper and allow to cool slightly before serving.

MINI TOAD-IN-THE-HOLE

If you don't have a Yorkshire pudding tin (pan) with four 10 cm/4 in compartments, use a bun tin to make eight small Yorkshire puddings and cook for slightly less time.

MAKES 4 BABY PORTIONS

⊛	METRIC	IMPERIAL	AMERICAN
Sausages	225 g	8 oz	8 oz
White vegetable fat (shortening)	15 g	½ oz	1 tbsp
Mixed vegetables, such as carrots, broccoli or courgettes (zucchini), cut into bite-sized chunks	100 g	4 oz	4 oz
Plain (all-purpose) flour	50 g	2 oz	½ cup
A pinch of salt			
Egg	1	1	1
Milk	175 ml	6 fl oz	¾ cup

① Cut the sausages into 3 cm/1¼ in slices. Use the white fat to lightly grease the compartments of a four-hole Yorkshire pudding tin, then divide the sausage slices between them.

② Cook the vegetables in boiling water or steam for 2–3 minutes or until almost tender. Drain well.

③ Put the Yorkshire pudding tin in a preheated oven at 220°C/425°F/gas mark 7 for 5 minutes. This will heat the tin and start cooking the sausages.

④ Meanwhile, sift the flour and salt into a bowl and make a well in the centre. Break the egg into the well, then pour in half the milk. Gradually mix the flour into the liquid to make a smooth batter, then whisk in the remaining milk.

⑤ Divide the vegetables between the compartments of the tin and pour over the batter. Bake on the top shelf in the oven for 30 minutes or until well risen and golden brown.

⑥ Remove from the tin and allow to cool for a few minutes before serving. Children may find them easier to eat with their fingers, rather than a knife and fork.

STRAWBERRY WOBBLE

Most children enjoy jelly (jello), so try turning it into a nutritious dessert with the addition of evaporated milk.

MAKES 2 BABY PORTIONS

✦	METRIC	IMPERIAL	AMERICAN
Packet of strawberry jelly	½	½	½
Can of evaporated milk	175 g	6 oz	I small
A few fresh strawberries, hulled and quartered, to decorate (optional)			

① Cut the jelly into small cubes. Pour over 120 ml/4 fl oz/ ½ cup of boiling water and stir until the jelly has dissolved. Leave to cool for 10 minutes.

② Stir in the evaporated milk and pour into two small bowls or jelly moulds. Leave to cool completely, then transfer to the fridge and chill until set.

③ Serve in the bowl or dip one of the moulds briefly into very hot water and turn out on to a plate to serve. Decorate with a few fresh strawberries, if liked.

④ Store the remaining portion in the fridge for up to 24 hours.

BAKED MAPLE APPLES

Although cooking (tart) apples are traditionally used for baking, eating (dessert) apples are much sweeter and a better size for a toddler to tackle.

MAKES 2 BABY PORTIONS

	METRIC	IMPERIAL	AMERICAN
Raisins	30 ml	2 tbsp	2 tbsp
Apple juice or water	75 ml	5 tbsp	5 tbsp
Small eating (dessert) apples	2	2	2
Butter or margarine, softened	15 g	½ oz	1 tbsp
Maple syrup	30 ml	2 tbsp	2 tbsp
A small pinch of ground cinnamon			
Ice cream, to serve			

① Put the raisins in a small bowl with the apple juice or water and leave to soak for at least 20 minutes.

② Core the apples and prick the skins with a fork or skewer in several places to prevent them from bursting. Put the apples in a small, shallow ovenproof dish.

③ Mix the butter or margarine, maple syrup and cinnamon together. Remove the raisins from the apple juice and stir into the mixture. Spoon into the centre of each apple. Pour the remaining soaking liquid into the dish.

④ Cover the apples with a piece of greased foil and bake in a preheated oven at 180°C/350°F/gas mark 4 for 40 minutes or until the apples are very tender.

⑤ Scoop the pulp from one of the apples into a bowl and allow to cool slightly before serving with ice cream.

⑥ Allow the remaining apple to cool. Cover and keep in the fridge for up to 24 hours.

RICH CHOCOLATE PUDDING

During cooking, this delicious dessert separates into two layers; a thick chocolate sauce at the bottom, topped with a fudgy sponge.

MAKES 2 ADULT PLUS 1 BABY PORTION

	METRIC	IMPERIAL	AMERICAN
Butter or margarine	50 g	2 oz	¼ cup
Caster (superfine) sugar	50 g	2 oz	¼ cup
Egg, beaten	1	1	1
Self-raising (self-rising) flour	40 g	1½ oz	⅓ cup
Cocoa (unsweetened chocolate) powder	15 g	½ oz	1 tbsp
Baking powder	2.5 ml	½ tsp	½ tsp
Vanilla essence (extract)	1.5 ml	¼ tsp	¼ tsp
Milk	15 ml	1 tbsp	1 tbsp
For the sauce:			
Light muscovado sugar	40 g	1½ oz	3 tbsp
Cocoa powder	15 g	½ oz	1 tbsp
Cold water	120 ml	4 fl oz	½ cup

① Cream the butter or margarine and sugar together until light and fluffy. Gradually add the egg, beating well after each addition. Sift the flour, cocoa powder and baking powder over the mixture. Add the vanilla essence to the milk and gently fold in.

② Spoon the mixture into a well greased 600 ml/1 pint/ 2½ cup ovenproof dish and level the top with the back of a spoon.

③ For the sauce, mix the muscovado sugar and cocoa powder together and sprinkle over the sponge mixture. Carefully pour over the cold water.

④ Bake in a preheated oven at 190°C/375°F/gas mark 5 for 30–35 minutes or until the pudding is risen and firm to the touch.

⑤ Spoon the baby portion of sponge and sauce into a bowl and allow to cool slightly before serving.

HOME-MADE ICE CREAM

MAKES 8 BABY PORTIONS

❄	METRIC	IMPERIAL	AMERICAN
Milk	300 ml	½ pint	1¼ cups
Egg yolks	3	3	3
Caster (superfine) sugar	50 g	2 oz	¼ cup
Cornflour (cornstarch)	2.5 ml	½ tsp	½ tsp
Vanilla essence (extract)	2.5 ml	½ tsp	½ tsp
Whipping cream	300 ml	½ pint	1¼ cups

① Pour the milk into a saucepan and heat to boiling point. Meanwhile, whisk the egg yolks, sugar, cornflour and vanilla essence together in a bowl until thick and creamy. Gradually whisk in the hot milk, then pour back into the pan.

② Cook the custard over a low heat, stirring all the time, until thick enough to coat the back of a wooden spoon. Do not allow to boil. Pour into a bowl, cover with a piece of dampened greaseproof (waxed) paper to prevent a skin forming and leave to cool.

③ Whisk the cream until just thick, then fold it into the cold custard. Pour into a shallow container and freeze, whisking two or three times during freezing to break down the ice crystals. Alternatively, churn in an ice cream maker.

④ Scoop the ice cream into bowls and allow to soften slightly at room temperature before serving.

Tip: Ice cream that has softened should never be refrozen, or you could risk food poisoning.

STRAWBERRY ICE CREAM

Purée 225 g/8 oz of strawberries in a food processor with 45 ml/3 tbsp of icing (confectioners') sugar. Rub through a sieve (strainer) to remove the pips, then stir into the cold custard.

CHOCOLATE ICE CREAM

Stir 75 g/3 oz of milk chocolate drops into the hot custard.

ICED RASPBERRY AND BANANA YOGHURT

MAKES 6 BABY PORTIONS

	METRIC	IMPERIAL	AMERICAN
Raspberries	225 g	8 oz	8 oz
Medium ripe banana	1	1	1
Soft light brown sugar	25 g	1 oz	2 tbsp
Plain Greek yoghurt	150 ml	¼ pint	⅔ cup

① Reserve a few raspberries for decorating, then put the rest in a food processor with the banana and sugar and purée until smooth. Press through a sieve (strainer) to remove the pips.

② Stir the yoghurt into the fruit purée. Pour into a shallow container and freeze, whisking two or three times during freezing to break up the ice crystals. Alternatively, churn in an ice cream maker.

③ Scoop into bowls and allow to soften slightly at room temperature before serving decorated with a few fresh raspberries.

CHEESE COOKIES

MAKES 12

❄	METRIC	IMPERIAL	AMERICAN
Self-raising (self-rising) flour	75 g	3 oz	¾ cup
Plain (all-purpose) wholemeal flour	25 g	1 oz	¼ cup
Ground rice	50 g	2 oz	⅓ cup
A pinch of salt			
Soft margarine	100 g	4 oz	½ cup
Cheddar cheese, finely grated	50 g	2 oz	½ cup

① Put all the ingredients in a mixing bowl and stir together with a wooden spoon until combined. Knead on a lightly floured work surface for a few seconds until smooth, then shape into a roll about 15 cm/6 in long. Wrap in clingfilm (plastic wrap) and chill in the fridge for 1 hour.

② Cut the roll into slices 1 cm/½ in thick and place on a lightly greased baking (cookie) sheet. Bake in a preheated oven at 190°C/375°F/gas mark 5 for 12–15 minutes or until lightly browned.

③ Leave to cool on the baking sheet for 5 minutes, then transfer to a wire cooling rack. When cold, store in an airtight tin for up to a week, or pack into a freezerproof bag or container and freeze until required.

BANANA CAKE WITH FUDGE FROSTING

MAKES 9 SQUARES

✤	METRIC	IMPERIAL	AMERICAN
Plain (all-purpose) flour	100 g	4 oz	1 cup
Baking powder	2.5 ml	½ tsp	½ tsp
Bicarbonate of soda (baking soda)	2.5 ml	½ tsp	½ tsp
Egg	1	1	1
Golden (light corn) syrup	15 ml	1 tbsp	1 tbsp
Milk	100 ml	3½ fl oz	scant ½ cup
Sunflower oil	60 ml	4 tbsp	4 tbsp
Ripe banana, mashed	1	1	1
For the fudge frosting:			
Butter or margarine	25 g	1 oz	2 tbsp
Milk	10 ml	2 tsp	2 tsp
Vanilla essence (extract)	1.5 ml	¼ tsp	¼ tsp
Cocoa (unsweetened chocolate) powder	15 ml	1 tbsp	1 tbsp
Icing (confectioners') sugar	175 g	6 oz	1 cup

①   Grease and line a 18 cm/7 in square tin (pan) with greaseproof (waxed) paper. Sift the flour, baking powder and bicarbonate of soda into a mixing bowl.

②   Beat the egg, golden syrup, milk, oil and banana together. Make a well in the middle of the dry ingredients and pour in the banana mixture. Beat together until mixed, then pour into the prepared tin.

③   Bake on the middle shelf of a preheated oven at 160°C/325°F/gas mark 3 for 25 minutes or until springy to the touch. Turn out on to a wire rack and leave to cool.

④   For the frosting, gently heat the butter or margarine, milk and vanilla essence in a small pan until melted. Sift the cocoa powder and icing sugar into a bowl and stir in the warm melted butter or margarine mixture. Beat together until light and fluffy.

⑤   Spread the frosting over the top of the cake. Cut into squares to serve. Store in an airtight container for up to 3 days.

YOGHURT AND RAISIN MUFFINS

MAKES 12

✳	METRIC	IMPERIAL	AMERICAN
Raisins	50 g	2 oz	⅓ cup
Orange juice	45 ml	3 tbsp	3 tbsp
Plain (all-purpose) flour	225 g	8 oz	2 cups
Baking powder	7.5 ml	1½ tsp	1½ tsp
Bicarbonate of soda (baking soda)	5 ml	1 tsp	1 tsp
Ground cinnamon	2.5 ml	½ tsp	½ tsp
A pinch of salt			
Light brown soft sugar	50 g	2 oz	¼ cup
Fine oatmeal	50 g	2 oz	½ cup
Egg	1	1	1
Milk	120 ml	4 fl oz	½ cup
Plain Greek yoghurt	250 ml	8 fl oz	1 cup
Butter or margarine, melted and cooled	40 g	1½ oz	3 tbsp

① Put the raisins in a small bowl, spoon over the orange juice and leave to soak for 1 hour. Line a 12-section muffin tin (pan) with paper muffin cases.

② Sift the flour, baking powder, bicarbonate of soda, cinnamon and salt into a mixing bowl. Stir in the sugar and oatmeal. Make a well in the middle.

③ Beat the egg with the milk. Stir in the soaked raisins, yoghurt and butter or margarine. Add to the dry ingredients. Stir briefly until just mixed.

④ Divide the mixture equally between the muffin cases. Bake in a preheated oven at 200°C/400°F/gas mark 6 for 20 minutes, until well risen and firm.

⑤ Cool the muffins on a wire rack. Remove the paper cases before serving warm or cold. Store in an airtight tin for up to 3 days or pack into a freezerproof container and freeze.

ICED CARROT CAKE

See the information on allergies on page 16 before using ground almonds for your baby.

MAKES 9 SQUARES

❄	METRIC	IMPERIAL	AMERICAN
Butter or margarine, softened	100 g	4 oz	½ cup
Soft light brown sugar	100 g	4 oz	½ cup
Eggs, beaten	2	2	2
Self-raising (self-rising) flour	75 g	3 oz	¾ cup
Baking powder	2.5 ml	½ tsp	½ tsp
Ground mixed (apple-pie) spice	1.5 ml	¼ tsp	¼ tsp
Milk	15 ml	1 tbsp	1 tbsp
Ground almonds	25 g	1 oz	¼ cup
Carrots, coarsely grated	150 g	5 oz	5 oz
For the icing (frosting):			
Mascarpone cheese	150 g	5 oz	5 oz
Orange juice	15 ml	1 tbsp	1 tbsp
Icing (confectioners') sugar, sifted	15 ml	1 tbsp	1 tbsp

① Grease and line a 18 cm/7 in square tin (pan). Cream the butter or margarine and sugar until pale and fluffy. Add the eggs a little at a time, beating well after each addition.

② Sift the flour, baking powder and mixed spice over the mixture and fold in with the milk and ground almonds. Finally, fold in the grated carrot.

③ Turn the mixture into the prepared tin and level the top with the back of a spoon. Bake in a preheated oven at 180°C/350°F/gas mark 4 for 35 minutes or until well risen and firm. Leave in the tin for 5 minutes, then turn out on to a wire rack to cool.

④ For the icing, beat the Mascarpone, orange juice and icing sugar together until smooth. Spread over the top of the cake. Cut the cake into squares and store in the fridge until ready to serve, or open-freeze, then wrap individual portions in clingfilm (plastic wrap) and freeze until required.

INDEX